Dedicated to the heroic people
in our police and fire departments,
whose value will always exceed
anything any of us could ever afford to pay.

Other Works by ALAN WEISS

Books

The Ultimate Consultant Series:

How to Establish a Unique Brand in the Consulting Profession (2001)
The Ultimate Consultant (2001)

*How to Sell New Business and Expand Existing Business in Professional
Service Firms* (2001)
Getting Started in Consulting (2000)
The Unofficial Guide to Power Management (2000)
How to Market, Establish a Brand, and Sell Professional Services (2000)
Good Enough Isn't Enough (1999)
How to Write a Proposal That's Accepted Every Time (1999)
Money Talks (1998)
Million Dollar Consulting (1992; rev. ed. 1998, 2002)
Our Emperors Have No Clothes (1995)
Best Laid Plans (1991)
Managing for Peak Performance (1990)
The Innovation Formula (with Mike Robert, 1988)

Booklets

How to Maximize Fees
Raising the Bar
Leadership Every Day
Doing Well by Doing Right
Rejoicing in Diversity

Audiocassettes

Peak Performance
The Consultant's Treasury
The Odd Couple®

Videos

Stories I Could Never Tell: Alan Weiss Live and Uncensored
Alan Weiss on Marketing
Alan Weiss on Product Development

Newsletters

Balancing Act: Blending Life, Work, and Relationships (electronic)
The Consultant's Craft
What's Working in Consulting (editor)

About the Author

Alan Weiss began his own consulting firm, Summit Consulting Group, Inc., out of his home in 1985 after being fired by a boss with whom he shared a mutual antipathy. Today, he still works out of his home, having traveled to fifty-one countries and forty-nine states, published fifteen books and over four hundred articles, and consulted with some of the great organizations in the world, developing a seven-figure practice in the process.

His clients have included Merck, Hewlett-Packard, Federal Reserve Bank, State Street Corp., Fleet Bank, Coldwell Banker, Merrill Lynch, American Press Institute, Chase, Mercedes-Benz, GE, American Institute of Architects, Arthur Andersen, and over two hundred similar organizations. He delivers fifty keynote speeches a year and is one of the stars of the lecture circuit. He appears frequently in the media to discuss issues pertaining to productivity and performance and has been featured in teleconferences, video conferences, and Internet conferences.

His Ph.D. is in organizational psychology, and he has served as a visiting faculty member at Case Western Reserve, St. John's, and half a dozen other major universities. He currently holds an appointment as adjunct professor in the graduate school of business at the University of Rhode Island, where he teaches a highly popular course on advanced consulting skills. His books have been translated into German, Italian, and Chinese.

The New York Post has called him "one of the most highly regarded independent consultants in the country," and *Success Magazine,* in an editorial devoted to his work, cited him as "a worldwide expert in executive education."

Dr. Weiss resides with his wife of thirty-four years, Maria, in East Greenwich, RI.

Contents

CHAPTER 3

The Basics of Value-Based Fees   37

It's Better to Be an Artist than to Be an Engineer

CHAPTER 4

How to Establish Value-Based Fees   57

If You Read Only One Chapter . . .

Introduction

The *Ultimate Consultant Series* is intended for successful practitioners who are seeking to scale still loftier heights. I'm happy to be among them.

This book is probably on the topic most eagerly anticipated of any I've written about in consulting. For the first time, I've recorded everything I know about the techniques that have worked best for me in raising fees, creating fees from unlikely sources, and supporting continuing fees. Yet this is by no means a mercenary book.

I believe in two aspects of consulting very strongly. First, you can't help others until you help yourself. Consequently, unless you're at least comfortable and secure financially, it's difficult to engage in pro bono work, to contribute to charities, and to help others to achieve their goals. Second, the basis for any successful client relationship is a win/win dynamic, the "good deal" you'll read about throughout this book. Therefore, you have to be treated well financially, and the client has to appreciate your value.

And when you come right down to it, there's a third aspect: Clients truly believe that they get what they pay for. No buyer ever bragged about being successful in capturing the cheapest consultant available, someone sitting by the phone with no business who took on the assignment in return for food. No, buyers—and their egos—revel in telling people that they snagged a consultant impossible to obtain, had to pay dearly, and expect everyone to listen closely.

After I worked on a project for a total of about six hours, the CEO asked his top officers what they would have charged had they been I. They guessed about $2,000 or less, having multiplied and divided by the $150 or $200 hourly rate that they charged.

"Well," said the CEO, "he's charging us *eighteen thousand dollars, so listen up!!*"

Dizzy Dean said once, "If you can do it, it ain't braggin.'" As you read on, you might want to listen up.

Alan Weiss, Ph.D.
East Greenwich, RI
November 2001

Acknowledgments

My thanks to the people who have made the fees possible: the wonderful clients with whom I've had the good fortune to work over the past sixteen years. I immodestly think that they're better off, and I know that I am. They are wonderful people.

Who says that nice guys finish last?

Here's to the most enduring: Dr. William Winter, Keith Darcy, George Rizk, Art Strohmer, Jarvis Coffin, Marilyn Martiny, Wayne Cooper, Lowell Anderson, Roseann Strichnoth, and Jerry Arbarbanal.

Deep appreciation to the wonderful editors at Jossey-Bass/Pfeiffer, headed by Kathleen Dolan Davies, the only human who speaks even faster than I do. It's been a joy to work with them all.

Once again to L.T. Weiss, my love and affection.

The Concept of Fees

Will People Actually Give Me Their Money for My Advice?

A fee is remuneration provided in return for perceived value received. I'm now tempted to say "End of Chapter 1."

The concept of providing a fee for services is a very old historical event that probably began in earnest with the end of subsistence farming. Once people had the knowledge and even primitive technology to grow more food than they could personally consume, they created the first medium for a fee: surplus goods of perceived value (food, of course, being of immense value to people who are hungry). The farmer could now acquire goods and services that could not be produced personally due to lack of time, lack of knowledge, and lack of tools.

Consequently, a class of people arose who could not or chose not to farm, but could earn their food through providing such goods and services. Some people provided things directly relevant to farming: tools, seeds, animals. But others provided for more personal needs: furniture, clothing, medicines. Still others, however, provided for the more conceptual needs: education, amusement, music.

It was only a matter of time before consultants were offering advice in return for food. You don't believe me? Every early potentate and satrap had court advisors, ranging from astrologers to fortune tellers, from high priests to military experts. Some day archeologists will unearth the pyramid that houses the thousands of consultants who guided that entire construction project. Their fees just might have been immortality.

My point is that people have been receiving fees in return for advice in one way, shape, or form for millennia, so we shouldn't be tentative or hesitant about the process here in the 21st Century.

THE ETHICAL NATURE OF CAPITALISM

We live in a capitalistic society. It is apparently a creaky system that happens to work far better than others, since in our lifetimes we've seen it grow to be the dominant economic configuration in the world. The exchange of goods and services for some form of remuneration, with a minimum of government interference or arbitrary regulation, is the system within which we live.[1]

Capitalism is based on a highly ethical set of premises: You agree to deliver a product or service of an agreed on quality at a certain time and in a certain condition; in return, I agree to provide certain remuneration in a specified amount on a particular date. That sounds simple, but it's actually the basis for all of our transactions involving the exchange of value for compensation.

Russia has failed (at least thus far) at capitalism, not because of an underlying or lingering communist belief system and not because of a lack of resources or unwilling populace. It has failed because the ethical basis required for the system to work is not firmly in place. There is still too much of an attitude of "Can I get away with this?" and "How can I take advantage of the other party?" We can also see this situationally within some professions, within certain industries, and within some organizations.

---

[1]Of course, capitalism is far better for generating wealth than for distributing wealth, which is why communism, socialism, and other mechanisms of state control have been popular (or at least tolerated) at various times. But they wind up creating an even worse class system, a fact to which any communist state, from the old Soviet Union to the lingering Cuba, can attest.

> Fees are actually dependent on only two things: Is there perceived value for the services provided that justifies the fee, and do both parties possess the intent of acting ethically?

For a consultant, the questions are about value, *not about fees.* Fees are dependent on value provided in the perception of the buyer and on the intent of the buyer and the consultant to do the right thing—to act ethically. The consultant, who provides what is often nothing more than advice—comments in the buyer's ear—must be diligent to ensure that the buyer perceives the value of the advice and will act properly upon receiving it (pay the bill, preferably early).

The mistakes consultants make about fees at the conceptual, strategic, and 35,000-foot level are these:

- Failing to understand that *perceived value* is the basis of the fee, and consequently attempting to manage (lower) the fee rather than manage (raise) the value.
- Failing to translate the importance of their advice into long-term gains for the client *in the client's perception,* and therefore believing that they must base their value on deliverables, time, and materials, which are actually low-value commodities.
- Failing to create a relationship with a legitimate, economic buyer,[2] meaning that the client may not do the right thing ethically (delay payment, argue about your value, arbitrarily change objectives).
- Failing to have the courage and belief system that support the high value delivered to the client, thereby reducing fees to a level commensurate with the consultant's own low self-esteem. That's right, consultants, not clients, are the main cause of low consulting fees.

---

[2]See my earlier works, *Million Dollar Consulting* (McGraw-Hill), *Getting Started in Consulting* (Wiley), and *The Ultimate Consultant* (the first book in this series) for more discussion about identifying and reaching economic buyers.

One of the main causes for failing to create a perception of perceived value is that the consultant doesn't appreciate that value. Since there are no "consulting schools" and not even an objective certification or licensing process for consultants, there is also no canon of consulting performance or behavior. Over 80 percent of the consultants I've met[3] fail to obtain a statement of value from the buyer relative to the success of the project. In other words, consultants are focused on the input side of the equation, trying to determine numbers of billable hours and just what that hourly rate can be, rather than focused on the output side: What will the project accomplish in terms of business goals? What is my contribution to that lasting benefit? and What is the proper fee to be paid in exchange for that large contribution, which the buyer has already stipulated?

I suspect that, in the old days, the farmer would say to the teacher, "If you tutor my children once a week, I'll give you a chicken and a bag of grain." Even today, the government says to the teacher, "Teach the community's children, and here's what we'll pay you" (not really much more than a chicken and a bag of grain, taking account of inflation over two thousand years). But a consultant—the ultimate business teacher—should be saying to the client, "Here's the value we will create together, and here's your share, and here's my share." The problem is that too many consultants are still working for chicken feed.

> Establishing value with the client is key. If the focus is on fees and not on value, the client has taken control of the discussion, and the client's interests will never be on maximizing your fees.

Ethically, the transaction should be based on fair remuneration for fair value delivered. That early teacher wasn't providing a morning a week of teach-

---

[3]I've conducted a formal mentoring program for consultants around the world for over five years, so my experience base here is rather comprehensive. I've also consulted with some of the largest consulting firms in the world.

ing, but rather the opportunity for the farmer's children to escape the day-long drudgery of farming and the limited life it afforded (especially after technology made the need for children on the farm less vital and transient workers provided extra labor in exchange for food). What is the value of one's children escaping their parents' lowly lot, avoiding an impoverished life, and building a better future (and, perhaps, taking care of their parents with their future fortunes)? It's got to be worth at least two chickens.

THE POWER OF MBS: THE MERCEDES-BENZ SYNDROME

People believe they get what they pay for. Moreover, emotion makes them act, while logic only makes them think. Put those two immutable theorems together, and you have what I've termed the "Mercedes-Benz Syndrome" (MBS).

When people enter an auto showroom today, no matter at what economic strata, the salespeople don't launch into intricate pitches about the electronic fuel injection or the wonders of rack-and-pinion steering. They encourage the potential buyer to sit in the car and then they mention, with a straight face, "You really look good in that car!" Yes, and the more expensive the model, the cooler we tend to look.

No one needs a Mercedes-Benz for transportation. Not at that price level, they don't. But a car purchase is, after all, a life style statement, and a Mercedes can begin to look quite reasonable in that light. When women try on a new frock, the sales help always say, "That was made for you; it brings out your eyes!" Despite the fact that I've never understood why a woman wants her eyes brought out, this ploy is always effective, even though it's repeated 26,000 times every day in the same department. When a man orders wine at dinner, the captain *always* says in response, "Excellent choice!" as the guy preens in that complimentary glow. (Never mind that he ordered vinegar, or that May wasn't such a good month.)

Fees are based on perceived value. That perceived value is on the part of the buyer. Consequently, the buyer's perception of value is the first point of attack for a consultant who wishes to maximize income.

> Psychologically, people believe they get what they pay for. Consequently, there is tremendous power in helping the buyer to stipulate what his or her perception of value is from the project and helping to maximize that perception.

Consultants are almost always remiss in not obtaining some agreement from the buyer on the nature of the value of the results of the project. Sometimes, the consultant is too anxious to attempt to close the sale; sometimes the relationship isn't yet strong enough to do it; many times the consultant feels inferior and not enough of a peer to suggest it; sometimes the skills are missing; and often, it's plain sloth.

Here are some basic questions to use to help the buyer arrive at some measure of value for any given project. You don't need to ask these interrogation-style, but it is a good idea to have them written somewhere and work them conversationally into the discussion until you're comfortable that you've obtained a clear expression of value.

Eleven Questions for Establishing Value with the Buyer[4]

1. What will be the difference in your organization at the conclusion of this project?
2. What if you did nothing?
3. What if this project failed (or have these attempts failed in the past)?
4. What will you be able to do that you can't do now?
5. What will be the effect on revenues (sales, profits, market share, and so on)?
6. What will be the difference for your repute (image, standing, stature, and so on)?

---

[4]I'm tired of "top ten" lists, so here's an extra nine percent of value from me to you. Also note that these questions are useless unless applied with the economic buyer—the person capable of writing the check.

7. What are the three greatest impacts of the result of this project's success (people love to think in threes)?
8. What will your boss's reaction be to this success (even economic buyers have a boss)?
9. What will this mean to you personally?
10. What peripheral and secondary value do you see accruing to this project?
11. What will you be proudest of at the conclusion of the project?

You can create another eleven or forty-four. My point is that you have to be prepared to discuss value with the buyer very early, prior to discussing methodology, options, timing, or, heaven forfend, fees.

Another fascinating aspect of MBS is that buyers have egos, which can greatly affect the buying process if you allow them to (and you want to allow them to, believe me). No buyer in my experience has ever said, "Okay, we've managed to secure the cheapest consultant we can find for our sales development. He was sitting at home with nothing to do, waiting to go to his normal day job, but I've persuaded him to work with us for $250 a day. We can afford that much, so let's use him as best we can."

Buyers are much more apt to say this to the troops: "Listen up. I've hired the finest consultant in the country on sales development. She graciously agreed to postpone a vacation to be with us. She's very expensive, but worth every cent if we use her right. Now, pay close attention, and plan to work with her closely."

When a CEO is in trouble, that person will call either someone who has clearly helped in the past or, if no one comes to mind, will call a "name" or a "brand" such as McKinsey or Andersen. No CEO wants to appear before the board and introduce a consulting firm without a track record or without a recognizable name. The executive ego will not permit it. ("This person is taking advice from someone I've never heard of?") The same holds true for every buyer. People believe they get what they pay for (and with their careers and businesses, they want the best).

Consequently, are you providing the "image" that appeals to the MBS? Do your materials bespeak a successful consultant? Is your website something you can proudly reference? Is your appearance professional and that of a peer to the buyer? Intellectually, are you able to easily interact and even to "push back" to demonstrate value in the earliest meetings?

> Value is often a function of NOT agreeing, NOT being supportive, and NOT being a "yes" person. How willing are you to disagree, question basic premises, and refuse impossible expectations?

Finally, the MBS creates rising expectations, which means that the buyer is prone to improve his or her condition through perceived high value assistance. Why purchase a less expensive model when the (perceived) better one is only a few hundred dollars more per month on the lease payment? Why take a basic consulting approach when a more sophisticated one is available?

That presupposes that a more sophisticated one *is* available, meaning that higher fees will always depend on the buyer seeing a set of options. The ultimate consultant always provides options for the client's review, so that the buyer can determine just how much value is available in terms of differing investments.

A consultant asked me once, "Aren't we ethically compelled to provide every possible assistance to meet the client's objectives?" Unequivocally no. We must meet the client's objectives, but to do industry-wide benchmarking studies, or longitudinal analyses for two years, or 360° feedback on four levels of management represents value above and beyond merely meeting the objective of "increasing sales closing rates," for example.

Offer a client various "value packages" that help the buyer ascend the MBS ladder. Over the course of my entire career, buyers have chosen my least expensive option less than 10 percent of the time, and my most expensive option over 35 percent of the time.

THE IMPORTANCE OF BUYER COMMITMENT, NOT COMPLIANCE

I can prove anything on a double-axis chart,[5] but the matrix in Figure 1.1. happens to hold true.

As you can see in Figure 1.1, the ideal relationship occurs when buyer commitment to the project (and to you) is high *and* your fee is high. If buyer commitment is high and your fee is low, you are wasting an opportunity. If buyer

| | Fee | |
	Low	High
Commitment High	Wasted Opportunity	Reciprocal Value
Commitment Low	Apathy	No Sale

Figure 1.1. The Relationships Between Fees and Buyer Commitment

commitment is low and your fee is low, you will, at best, create an indifferent sale. And when fees are high but commitment is low, you will be shown the door.

My estimate is that most consultants' approaches (whether or not they actually get the business) are in the bottom, left quadrant about 25 percent of the time; in the bottom, right quadrant about 10 percent of the time; in the upper, left quadrant about 60 percent of the time; and in the upper, right quadrant only about 5 percent of the time!

That's right: Most consultants, including most of you reading this, habitually undercharge for your services and deliver far more than you are receiving in remuneration, considering your contribution to success. You are undercharging and over-delivering and, lest you think that to be an exalted position, consider trying to pay your mortgage or IRA contribution with that combination.

Most buyers *comply.* That is, they are willing to go along with the "expert," even if it's sometimes against their better judgment. Or they will delegate you to someone they believe has the technical ability to evaluate your proposition, typically in the human resources department, or finance, or legal. (Put these together and they are an anagram for "no business here.") Buyers who merely comply may be seen at first blush as "easy" to work with, but they are actually land mines waiting for some weight to trigger them. That's because they hold the consultant responsible for everything. They

---

[5]In fact, I've written a book with a subtitle, "Give Me a Double Axis Chart and I Can Rule the World" (*The Great Big Book of Process Visuals,* Las Brisas Research Press).

believe that *you* are doing something to them, or for them, or at them, but certainly not *with them.*

Compliance is dangerous because the buyer usually takes no inherent responsibility for the project, but rather abdicates to the consultant. I've never found a project that a consultant can unilaterally implement successfully, since consultants have responsibility but no real authority. (When that dynamic is reversed, it's the sign of a very poor implementation scheme.)

Consulting projects should be true partnerships between the consultant and the economic buyer. This begins prior to the proposal being signed and is an integral aspect of creating high fees. If the buyer is merely compliant, he or she will grudgingly or apathetically go along with the implementation, but will do so at the lowest possible fee. The buyer's head is involved, but not the gut (and logic makes people think, but emotion makes them act). Large fees are dependent on *emotional buy-in,* and that must be achieved in the relationship aspect of the consulting sequence, well prior to the actual closing of business.

This is why patience in formulating the right relationship is more important than attempting to make a "fast sale." The former is a partnership where fees are academic; the latter is a unilateral benefit where fees are often the main point of contention.

> The buyer's commitment to outcomes and to his or her role in the partnership being formed to reach those outcomes is the key determinant to high fees. Buyers who are too willing to go along with your recommendations are as potentially fatal as those who dig in their heels after you've said "hello."

CRITICAL STEPS FOR BUYER COMMITMENT

It's worth repeating here briefly the sequence of events in the consulting business acquisition process that engenders the highest quality commitment, the first three shown in the graphic in Figure 1.2 and explained below.

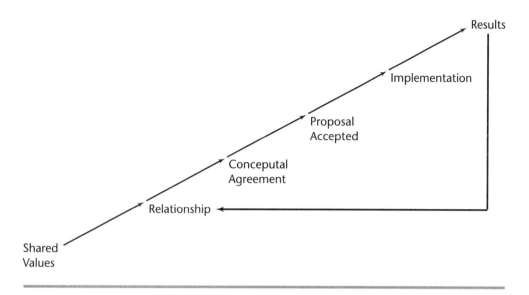

Figure 1.2. Consulting Business Acquisition Sequence

Shared Values. Those common business beliefs that will allow you to work effectively with the prospect, for example, a mutual antipathy for downsizing or a common belief in the importance of ongoing employee feedback.

Relationship. That level of interaction in which you and the buyer are comfortable with each other, can be honest (even in disagreeing), and share insights and assistance with each other on a mutual basis.

Conceptual Agreement. Agreement between you and the buyer on:

- Objectives for the project, expressed as business outcomes
- Metrics, measures of success toward those objectives
- Value, the buyer's stipulation of how he or she and the organization will be better off as a result of those objectives being met

These three critical steps, which are each dependent on the prior being successfully in place—addressed in detail in Chapters 3 and 4—will garner buyer commitment. The absence of conceptual agreement will result in either a lost sale or a lousy sale (and the latter is often more damaging than the former).

Fees are dependent on buyer commitment well before a proposal is ever tendered. Note that fees are not even on my chart.

THE BUOYANCY OF BRANDS: HOW BRANDS HELP FEES

The second book in this series was dedicated to branding for consultants. One of the key reasons for effective branding is to enhance fees.

Fees are (or should be) based on value. That value is always in the eye of the beholder, in our case, the economic buyer. Hence, the more value conveyed to that buyer by the most powerful means, the less downward pressure on fees. Effective branding actually creates a fee "buoyancy."

> There is actually one thing better than a buyer impressed by you and respecting you on sight, and that is the buyer impressed by you and respecting you before ever laying eyes on you.

No CEO ever said, "Get McKinsey in here," when strategy work was needed, then followed up by saying, "I think they're too expensive." As they say in the Ferrari showroom when someone asks about gas mileage, "If that's your concern, you really shouldn't be here."

Ferrari is a brand that evokes certain immediate understandings on the part of the potential individual buyer:

- High cost
- Top status
- High maintenance
- High insurance
- High repairs
- Unique image
- Personal ego needs met

You know those things going in, and they are not points for discussion when dealing with a salesperson.

Similarly, McKinsey is a brand that evokes certain immediate understandings on the part of the potential corporate buyer:

- High cost (fees will not be negotiable)
- Top status (no one can say we're giving this short shrift)
- High maintenance (a lot of junior partners will appear)
- High insurance (the board can't complain about quality of the help)
- High repairs (they will recommend tough interventions)
- Unique image (the cachet alone will raise expectations)
- Personal ego needs met (only the best for the best)

You get my point: The mere power of a brand is sufficient to overcome any resistance to fees and, in fact, often elevates fees merely by dint of association with such brand images as quality, repute, client history, media attention, and so on.

There is no brand as powerful as your name, although strong company brands can also serve quite well. When a potential client says, "Get me Jane Jones" or "Get me The Teambuilder," that client is articulating a clear imperative: Don't go shopping, don't compare prices, don't issue a request for proposals; just get me that person I've heard so much about.

If you refer back to the Mercedes-Benz Syndrome above, brands create an upward expectation of *both* quality and commensurate fees. No one expects an outstanding person to come cheap. In the MBS, you usually have to convince the buyer of that quality through careful relationship building. But a strong brand shortcuts that process considerably. The relationship building still needs to be done (for reasons of commitment, noted above), but the time required is significantly reduced. The buyer wants to be a partner, wants to follow your suggestions, and wants to participate *because your credibility has preceded you.*

Brands are accelerators of credibility and, therefore, of relationships. They immediately justify higher fees *in the mind of the buyer,* and that is the only mind that counts on that matter.

It's not the intent of this book to explore how to create a brand.[6] However, it is vital to understand brand importance in the fee-setting process. Like bank loans being hard to acquire when you need them and easy to obtain when you no longer need them, high fees are most difficult when no one has ever heard of you and you desperately need the income and easiest when you're well-known and business is rolling in.

The crime here is that many successful consultants either don't bother to use their past success to create effective brands or have created brands that they don't properly leverage for higher fees. Tom Clancy has never written a book nearly as good as his original, *The Hunt for Red October,* but he's certainly been paid far more for every subsequent work than for that first effort. He has been a smart marketer and a hugely successful "brand" (to the extent that he hasn't even written some work he's paid for, but simply inserts "Tom Clancy" on the cover and it's sufficient).

Brands create higher fees. And higher fees enable you to solidify the credibility of your brand.

CREATING SHARED SUCCESS

Many consultants prefer to take a position (or don't know any better) of "Here's how I'm going to improve things around here." The success is the consultant's, a sort of largesse provided for the lucky client. There is a certain power in being "the expert" without whom all goes to hell, but there is a huge risk, although not the one that might be apparent.

The apparent risk is that the client might not benefit as desired or, heaven forfend, might actually suffer a reversal of fortune. Remember the physician's sage credo, "First, do no harm." It's no accident that large consulting firms are being sued right and left in this litigious society. They have not "delivered" the desired results.

However, the greater risk is that, even with demonstrable success, the buyer feels alienated, disenfranchised, and apart from it. The fee in this case, despite success, will be a grudging one. For one thing, the client is now fearful of long-term dependence and doesn't want to incur huge costs each time the

---

[6]But do feel free to read the prior book in this series, *How to Establish a Unique Brand in the Consulting Profession* (Jossey-Bass/Pfeiffer, 2001).

consultant's "expertise" is required to solve another problem. For another, the buyer does not feel an intrinsic ownership and sense of well-being that would emotionally overwhelm any reservations about costs. Third, from an ego perspective, the buyer will feel the need to insert some leverage into the relationship that permits the buyer to feel the continuing upper hand and reminds the consultant that he or she serves at the buyer's pleasure (especially if the results are so visible that others in the organization are talking about them).

> True partners never begrudge each other their proper due. In fact, there's an implicit trust that neither partner will take advantage of the other and that terms, conditions, and time frames are innately fair.

Fee pressure decreases with a sense of shared investment, shared accountabilities, and shared success. Figure 1.3 shows the difference between a focus on a buyer and seller (top) who are locked into a battle over costs with only vague benefits established and two partners (bottom) who have agreed on tangible results where the fee is simply an intelligent and economical investment.

When the buyer simply views the consultant as another vendor providing certain expertise, then the cost of acquisition becomes the key focus, because

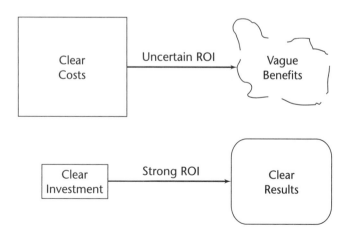

Figure 1.3. Costs from the Expert vs. Investment from the Partner

this is a commodity purchase (Who can provide the cheapest computer monitors per our specifications?). However, when the buyer's self-image and role are as a partner in the consulting process, then the decision becomes one of return on investment, and the clearer the outcomes (see "conceptual agreement" above) and the more dramatic, the higher the investment that is justified.

This is particularly true when that investment includes the buyer and key organization people as a part of the partnership. Some of the most successful consulting projects I've landed—and those most impervious to fee pressure—are those in which a "virtual consulting team" was formed comprising key client resources and me. There is no way that an educated buyer wants to underfund or "hedge" on that investment.

The key factors in shared success include:

- A "we" mentality from the first contact with the prospect
- Literature, websites, and promotional materials that talk about partnering and shared responsibilities
- A formal description of "joint accountabilities" in the proposal itself[7]
- A strong focus on outcomes and business results, not on tasks or deliverables
- Ample opportunity for the buyer and other key people to take credit and to bask in the success
- Candor in tackling inevitable problems and setbacks

Err on the side of the client and buyer receiving more accolades for success than you. But also err on the side of higher fees and faster payment of those fees. That's the quid pro quo.

It really doesn't matter what the organization believes. What matters is what the current and future buyer(s) believes. The danger of consultants trying to "do it alone" is that the client runs through this sequence:

---

[7]See the author's *How to Write a Proposal That's Accepted Every Time* (Kennedy Information, 1999).

1. Who's John Adams?
2. Get me that guy John Adams.
3. Get John Adams.
4. Get John Adams if you can.
5. Get someone close to John Adams.
6. Get me a young John Adams.
7. Who's John Adams?

In a true partnership that focuses on shared success, however, no buyer will try to eliminate one half of the successful combination.

CHAPTER 1 ROI (THE SUMMARY)

- One has to develop a philosophy about fees. That is, they are not a "necessary evil" nor a "dirty part of the job," but rather a wonderful and appropriate exchange for the superb value you are delivering to the client. That exchange is eons old and represents the highest ethical canon of modern capitalism: agreed on payment for agreed on value.
- Buyers tend to believe that they get what they pay for, and higher fees actually portend higher quality for most buyers. They will also guarantee a higher level of buyer commitment, and that commitment, not compliance, is key to producing a return-on-investment (ROI) mentality, rather than a cost-reduction mentality.
- Brands tend to raise buyers' perception of quality still higher, which is why strategic marketing is an essential aspect of the ultimate consultant's repertoire.
- Finally, shared success—understood from the outset and achieved at the conclusion—is vital to the belief in consultant worth as part of a partnership with the buyer.

The One Percent Solution:[8] Believe in your own value and build your perceived value in demonstrable ways every day. That is the fuel for the acceleration of fees.

---

[8]Improve by 1 percent a day, and in just seventy days, you're twice as good.

CHAPTER 2

The Lunacy of Time and Materials Models

Who Wants to Be as Dumb as a Lawyer?

The historic manner in which consultants have billed for their services has been based on time units, usually hourly rates or per diem assessments. There is no logical reason for doing so, but the underlying reasons seem to have included:

- Other professionals had set a precedent, most notably lawyers and accountants, both of whom preceded consultants onto the business stage.[1] (Architects, designers, and other professionals also charge in this manner.)

---

[1]The first management consultant was probably Frederick Winslow Taylor, the founder of time and motion studies and the author of *Principles of Scientific Management* (which wasn't so scientific at all). He worked in the early part of the 20th Century, his oeuvre being published in 1911.

- Most of the conventional working trades have placed a premium on their time, for example, plumbers, electricians, carpenters, and so forth.
- Time is the universal objective, in that the client and the consultant can agree on the length of an hour or a day. (Of course, how much of that duration is spent on qualitative work is another matter entirely.)
- Consultants have had a ready-made lever for increasing their business by merely increasing their time investment.
- One's consulting worth was usually perceived as one and the same as one's physical presence, thereby attaching worth to "showing up." It was easy to attach a fee to that presumed worth: "If I'm here, I must be helping, so I ought to be paid."
- The uncertainty of the work required that the consultant "protect" future time by charging for all time spent, since there was no firm way of predicting how much time would be required, what new and unforeseen developments might impact the project, or what increasing demands the client might come up with. The belief was that time spent on one client was irretrievably lost and was therefore denied another client (and another client's potential fee).

> Since consultants offer advice for long-term enrichment, why charge for short-term visits? My recommendations are, fortunately, worth far more than my company.

Finally, there seems to be a widespread belief, unaccountably held to most dearly by the larger consulting firms, that the only consulting items of value are either time or materials (deliverables) and that clients wouldn't pay for anything as ephemeral as pure advice. Of course, stated that way, this proposition is true. The point, however, is that clients will pay a great deal for the *outcomes, results, and long-term value* of that advice.

And that value has nothing whatsoever to do with time.

SUPPLY AND DEMAND ILLOGIC

One of the worst pieces of advice I ever heard was from a professional speaker who pontificated to the audience that speakers should "raise fees when demand exceeds supply." That might work for soy beans or cement, but it's simply goofy when applied to professional services.

Demand *never* exceeds supply. Not only do I know of no consultants who are booked every day of the year, but I can't imagine one who would want to be. The idea, I always thought, was to work a minimal amount of time while earning a maximum amount of money. (My ideal client is one who pays me $5 million to work for twenty minutes a year. My wife points out that, if I can work for twenty minutes, I can certainly manage forty minutes.)

Moreover, supply and demand rest on the trembling foundation that a single client at a single time usurps all attention. It is possible to do something for multiple clients at any given time: research, joint meetings, newsletters, focus groups, interviews, and a plethora of other activities can benefit numerous clients in unique ways. (The lawyers achieve this by billing different clients for an aggregate of hours that only slightly exceeds the total number found in any one day by a factor of four.)

> The idea is to meet demand with a minimal supply of labor and, in fact, meet growing demand by an increasingly diminishing investment of time. This is called working smart, not hard.

There are actually formulas that advise that consultants do the following:

1. Determine the amount of money they need to support their total life style.
2. Calculate the total number of hours available to consult during a year, eliminating holidays, personal needs, etc.
3. Determine an approximate usage rate of the remaining time (for example, what percentage of time will the consultant probably be booked, given the marketplace and focus).
4. Divide the result of the usage rate applied to the net available hours by the life style needs total. This gives you the hourly rate needed to meet financial goals within the given time constraints.

Now, there are only about seventy or eighty things wrong with this, but I'll concentrate only on the relative few needed to thoroughly debunk this point of view.

First, it's absolutely nuts to use your current life style (or even an intended life style) as the basis for income needs. What about unanticipated expenses (illnesses, extended family needs, unexpected opportunities to invest, and so on)? Especially for younger consultants (or for anyone without fully funded, totally comfortable retirement savings), why delimit yourself during your highest potential earning years?

Second, how do you intelligently arrive at a number of hours you think are available? The number will always go *down* from that estimate, never up, meaning that your hourly rates will be inadequate and you'll either have to raise them or take more hours from "private time." Time is always usurped by the unforeseen, which, by definition one would think, can't be forecast.

Third, approximations of usage rates are absurd because high rates aren't necessarily good. It's simply not smart to be booked 80 percent or more of the time, because your flexibility is eliminated (just as any good medical consultant will tell a medical practice not to book all available hours every week, but to save time for emergencies and other exigencies). Wouldn't we all rather work less for fascinating clients who pay us well rather than more for dull clients who pay us poorly?

Fourth and finally, the resultant hourly rate in the equation above has no bearing on the market, the client need, the unique conditions, or the value of the help delivered. It reduces the consultant to an arbitrary commodity, to be compared to other hourly rates and other commodities, like fish or movie tickets. When you deliberately remove market uniqueness and differentiation, you also remove the basis for high fees.

> The last thing a good consultant wants to happen is for a client to make comparisons *not* based on the value of the contribution but rather based on the charge by the hour. Our value is simply not conveyed by merely showing up (thank goodness).

So the very basis for a "supply and demand" dynamic is fallacious. We do not have a limited supply of expertise, nor do we seek higher and higher demand (not if we want to maintain a life). What we should want to accomplish is an ideal relationship of interesting, growth-oriented work and fees based on our contribution to the client's results.

The "Big Five" (or whatever it is at this reading, having come down from the "Big Eight") consultancies are all the stepchildren of accounting and audit firms. Consequently, they have had a fixation on developing billing rates that are based on hours, fit nicely into boxes on a spreadsheet, and can be conveyed in a no-brain fee schedule. These are, after all, descendants of the primeval bean counter. Their dilemma, faced with tremendous overhead of multiple offices, advertising, and huge recruiting costs, has been addressed by creating an army of inexpensive technicians who descend on the client, with an hourly billing rate that is somehow digestible but significant enough to generate profit when multiplied by the legion of consultants assigned to the account. This model has been adopted by smaller firms and independent practitioners who, frankly, should know better.

Supply and demand tends to get way out of whack when the consulting firm can produce a prodigal supply of low level people, irrespective of the actual client demand. And this tactic has, understandably, driven clients to ask:

"Can you do this with fewer people?"
"Can you do this in fewer days?"
"Can you do this with cheaper people?"

These are not the questions we want a client to be asking. I'd rather hear a client ask:

"How can we maximize the results?"
"Will you work with me on this as a partner for as long as it takes?"
"Will you assure me access to you, personally?"

These latter questions represent the value of a long-term relationship, not an attempt to get me out before I run up too much of a bill.

Leave supply and demand to the economists or the people raising ostriches. It has less than nothing to do with good consultants, and it should never be used as a basis for fees.

ETHICAL CONFLICTS OF INTEREST AND OTHER SMALL MATTERS

Whenever a consultant accepts work on the basis of being paid for time spent on the project, an immediate conflict of interest arises. There is no way around this, the problem is always present, and it is caused by the following.

The Basis for Profit

The consultant only makes money when physically present or able to demonstrate that time is being expended somehow, somewhere for the client. This tends to compel the consultant to do the following:

- Maximize, not minimize, the number of physical activities (focus groups, interviews, observations, meetings, and so on)
- Accept peripheral assignments that may not be integral—or even important—to the actual project
- Encourage and not discourage scope creep, since there is no penalty for blurring the project boundaries
- Recommend non-essential tasks that don't contribute to results but do contribute to billable hours[2]

Value-based fees are far better *for the client* because they remove the ethical compromises that attend hourly or daily billing. You want the client to make a *single* ROI decision at the time of the proposal, and not a new ROI decision every day (or hour).

[2]I know there are many of you saying, "Yes, but honorable people wouldn't do that." Maybe, but I point out that honorable people regularly cheat on their taxes, cross the street against the light, and cheat the phone company, simply because the opportunities present themselves and the incorrect action is only a brief rationalization away (the phone company cheats me, what's the government done for me lately, there's no traffic that I can see or can't outrun). We need to eliminate temptations that lead to unethical behavior, not expect that everyone will act honorably.

The Client Need Quandary

The client has to make an investment decision, in effect, every time the consultant may be able to offer some help. Hence, a normal helping relationship is reduced to ROI concerns on even the most minor occasions:

- The client may decide that a $10,000 issue isn't worth $2,500 of consulting help, ignoring the fact that the consultant's expertise could help unearth the $400,000 issue underlying it.
- Subordinates are loath to use the consultant because approval is required from superiors for the additional fees, and the subordinates may not want to admit so readily that help is needed so frequently.
- Clients may forego legitimate, additional extensions of the project for purely cost considerations, even though work in those areas would add immeasurably to the client's betterment.

Conflicts with Client Purchasing Policies

Most organizations have policies for dealing with "vendors," and once you quote time-based fees you will become no less a vendor than the plumber or the computer repair guy.

- In putting yourself in the same category as other hourly vendors, you are asking the client to then treat you differently by not requiring a limit on hours and/or by not adhering to company hourly billing policies. ("We never pay trainers more than $2,500 per day." "But I'm not a trainer." "You're in the same category.")
- A good purchasing manager or vendor coordinator is paid to extract the best possible rates from vendors. Consequently, they will always try to minimize your time rates, and you will be in danger of pitting your corporate buyer against his or her own purchasing function.
- If the company accepts billing for hourly units, how do you conscientiously bill for portion of hours or quick phone responses? Do you emulate the legal practice of making everything a fifteen-minute minimum, even if the call takes two minutes? Do you aggregate them and somehow justify them on a time sheet? This is not all that far from fudging the numbers. (If you're doing research that benefits two clients, do you charge them each for the same half-day, or do you prorate it?)

Preserving Client Budgetary Limits

Almost any client will reasonably ask for some estimate of investment so that a proper budget can be allocated. Even with the most exacting formula, these are always only estimates, and the client's budget is actually endangered constantly.

- If, at a critical point in the project investigation, you and the client find an unforeseen critical need, how can the client appropriately budget more funds or preserve those already in place? Must you lower your hourly rate, or demand additional funds, or ignore the urgency?
- The client is too often forced into a Hobson's choice: Some priorities can be met, but not others as the hours and days build and the meter constantly ticks away at the fixed budget.
- If there is more than one budget involved among multiple buyers, how are the funds correctly allocated? If the actions of one department demand remedial work in another, which should be properly assessed and by how much? Not everyone is going to be happy with the decision.

> As projects unfold, something has to give: Either the client will have to come up with additional funds to pay for more hours, or the consultant will have to leave work undone (or do work for free). Why on earth get into that position?

There's one final ethical issue I want to discuss, which often doesn't arise as an ethical problem, but actually is one: the downward pressure on consulting fees when based on time and materials.

The client's natural compulsion will be to reduce one or both of the only two variables representing the buyer's costs: amount of time or amount of money per time unit. The consultant will be compelled to try to do the exact opposite. However, since the client is the only one who can say "yes," the buyer's determination will prevail. Three bad things immediately transpire:

1. The buyer and consultant are in an *adversarial* position, despite working together, presumably as partners, on the same goals. One is trying to minimize and the other is trying to maximize involvement. Yet the point should be active collaboration toward goals, not concern about the methodology or involvement to reach the goals.
2. The buyer will want to minimize time, requiring the consultant to use fewer resources, fewer visits, and/or a smaller scope. All of this may be highly detrimental to the quality of the investigation.
3. The buyer will want to minimize hourly rates, which forces the consultant to often make concessions. This, in turn:
   - Endangers the magic formula described above based on the consultant's earnings needs calculations
   - Tells the buyer that the consultant has "padded" the fees and prompts even the most benign of buyers to wonder "How low can he go?" (I can name that tune in two notes)

For legitimate ethical interests, for the client and the consultant, time and materials billing is problematic and compromising. Not *usually* compromising. *Always* compromising.

LIMITING PROFITS, OR WHY NOT JUST FORGET *DOMANI*

The very worst aspect of billing based on time is the limitation it places on profitability. I've never believed in business plans, for myself or for my clients, because the danger about a plan is that you might achieve it.[3]

Consultants—and this applies particularly aptly to solo practitioners—take extraordinary business risks. Why shouldn't they reap the commensurate rewards? The only intelligent business proposition is to attempt to maximize profitability. Note that I'm not saying "maximize business," because that might

---

[3]Of course, major organizations need business plans to show the shareholders that management is fiscally responsible, but they also put out beautiful annual reports that have nothing whatsoever to do with the actual business. No one should manage against a business plan for fear of hitting it and missing untold opportunities.

lead to harder work, longer hours, and an infringement on one's life balance. But I am saying "maximize profits" because we wouldn't be very good business people or consultants if we didn't.

Therefore, why create a straw man of an artificial business plan (Have you ever really seen managers in October still managing against a plan created the prior September?) that delimits growth? The mantra-like focus on "increasing business by 20 percent" or "gaining five new coaching clients" or "gaining 5 percent in the Canadian marketplace" is rather pointless if, in fact, the conditions were such that you should have increased by 40 percent, gained twelve new coaching clients, or become one of the major players in the Canadian market.

An hourly fee is a similar delimiting factor. You will always be at the mercy of the "cap" in your marketplace. (The best New York attorneys, senior partners, working for the best clients, are hard-pressed to go much above $500 an hour, and they represent a small fraction of all attorneys, the average income of which is about $88,000 in the U.S.) And the larger firms with junior help will always be able to undercut you with junior rates.

If I estimate that I can work forty weeks a year, and that I'll be "billable" an astonishing 80 percent of the time, that provides me with 1,280 hours (80 percent X 40 = 32 X 40 hours in a work week). At my New York lawyer maximum of $500 an hour, that comes to $640,000—not a bad year's work (although not anywhere close to the best solo practitioner consultants). However, a more reasonable rate is probably half that, resulting in $320,000, and a more reasonable billing percentage might be 60 percent, not 80 percent, resulting in $240,000. Now that's still not exactly shabby, but is that the number that will support your life style through marriage, children, tuition, retirement, care for elderly parents, vacations, investments, unexpected emergencies, and the pure *joie de vivre* of it all?

I think not. I tell my mentorees all the time that one hundred thousand dollars ain't what it used to be.

It is absolutely crazy to adapt any billing scheme that can place a cap on your income. Time unit billing does just that. The only good reason for deliberately making less money is the urge to work less, and even there I have a hard time believing that you must also make less money if you're smart.

Architects are (in)famous for their hourly billing, and they are probably the only profession which had a decrease in net income over the boom years of the mid-to-late 1990s.[4] They were done in by a number of factors, all within their own means to control, but particularly these:

- Hourly billing, which declined as hours declined due to competition from general contractors, engineers, and others who freely "poached" on architects' turf
- Fierce competition and resultant pressure on prices caused by a plethora of architects, not unlike today's burgeoning number of consultants (In Duluth, no less, a focus group told me, "Stop any three people on the street, and two of them are architects." I quickly termed this the "Duluth architect syndrome.")
- An absence of negotiation skills with educated buyers, meaning that the only variable the architects would manipulate was their own hourly fees, and always downward
- Blindness to the real profit margins caused by love of the profession (every architect wants to build a cathedral and keeps waiting for that contract, even though architects overwhelmingly are engaged in house extensions and garage additions. Consequently, they are always too willing to take on unprofitable projects to keep them busy "until the real thing comes along," and they tell you that they'll make up the shortfall "on volume."[5])

Consultants have been little better. The focus on "billable time" has driven both independents and large consulting operations to focus on work, use, and task, on the assumption that something is better than nothing—we can't let all those billable hours be spent sitting here at a desk, after all. This mentality severely limits profits because, like the architects, it drives one to work that

---

[4]The American Institute of Architects was a client for several years, and this was perhaps THE major concern of the association and the membership.

[5]One of the truly funniest skits I've ever seen was a pseudo-commercial on the NBC show "Saturday Night Live" in which the late Phil Hartman was a pitchman for a bank that only made change, nothing else, no loans, no mortgages, no investments, only change. "I know what you're wondering," he would deadpan into the camera. "How can we do it? The secret is one word: volume."

shouldn't be undertaken at rates that can't be countenanced. Something is *not* better than nothing. Some things are worse than nothing, because they cost you money.

Billable hours, and the formulas on which the more methodical base them, are pernicious and insidious dampeners of profit. Moreover, the need to be competitive on such a commodity ultimately forces downward pressure on all time unit rates. So in the tactical application—fees based on time for the project—the consultant will suffer from continuing downward pressure when played off on others offering the same commodity pricing, and in the strategic sense—using time units to create a year's living expenses—there will never be enough hours or a high enough rate to dramatically improve income.

Other than their tactical and strategic failure, time based fees are great.

WHY LAWYERS AND CPAS DO SO POORLY

The problem with professions that use time and materials charges is that the practitioners have no real appreciation for their own value and, hence, cannot adequately (much less dramatically) convey their value to the client. Some cases in point:

Attorneys

Lawyers have finally understood that their ultimate worth is not in their activity but in their result. Therefore, contingency fees have begun to proliferate. It's not uncommon for a law firm to take 30 percent or 40 percent (or even more in some conditions) of the total client settlement.

The problem is that the attorneys often take this, as they say at the craps tables in Las Vegas, as "betting on the come." This means that, if they lose the case, they not only fail to collect any fee, *but they are also out their legitimate legal expenses.* This is high stakes gambling, and it leads to at least four ethical quandaries:

1. Pushing the case beyond the plaintiff's patience or commitment, because, in for a dime in for a dollar, it's cheaper to invest more on the hope of a possible victory than to simply abandon all prior investment

2. Avoiding early settlements in the hope of hitting the jackpot of a huge jury decision or a more favorable last-minute settlement in the face of a damaging trial
3. Taking on cases of questionable legal merit and/or suing parties not really at fault but who have deep pockets and wealthy insurers
4. Desperate legal tactics to try to save a case at the last minute

> There isn't one profession using time units or percentages as billing bases that can match the potential fees of consultants using value-based fees. Not one.

Attorneys are locked into a terrible billing system that does not represent their true value to their clients (and is why they wind up billing $8.40 for duplicating and postage, so desperate are they to recoup costs).

Even on a more modest basis, effective and legally tight wills, estates, divorces, house closings, partnership agreements, and the myriad of other business aspects that lawyers undertake are worth a great deal to the beneficiary of such expertise. How much? Well, far more than a couple of hundred dollars an hour, that's for sure.

CPAs

Since these folks are fixated on neat boxes and clear rates as a professional pathology, it's not surprising that they cheat themselves out of their fair remuneration.

These are people who balance books, save tax dollars, highlight areas of enhanced profitability, set up effective retirement plans, provide investment advice, and generally help you exhaust every legal nook and cranny to keep your money where it belongs—in your own pocket. For the glory of providing this value, they charge $150 or so an hour.

CPAs don't get it (although more and more financial planners are beginning to). They see their value as tasks performed, which are tightly tied to and choreographed by time involved. They even have fee schedules of their various tasks, on the assumption that they can pretty accurately forecast the amount of hours needed for each task. And they probably can, which is neither here nor there.

I love the guy who does my taxes and financial planning, who may have saved me hundreds of thousands over the years (and kept me out of jail in the bargain). But I'm glad he doesn't read my books. Because if he did and decided to change his billing basis, I'd have no choice.

I'd have to pay him more.

Search Firms

I include these folks because they think they're smart and believe they've devised a billing basis that overcomes time units: a percentage of first-year compensation. (And some of these firms are contingency firms, not retainer firms, meaning they don't get paid unless they produce.)

I ask you to simply consider this: A search firm placed Lou Gerstner at IBM when that company was severely suffering. CEO Gerstner during his tenure increased the stock price, improved the value of the company, increased market share, increased both revenues and profitability, found new sources of lucrative business (for example, IBM consulting services), and provided a host of other important improvements. His net contribution to IBM well-being is in the billions of dollars.

And how was the foxy search firm paid that placed him at IBM? They received about a third of his first-year total compensation. Let's say that was as much as $500,000, which I doubt. Even so, is a half-million fair compensation for a consulting firm that produced billions of dollars in improvement? I wouldn't accept it. It seems to me that a hundred million or so is reasonable and cheap at twice the price.

> Taking a percentage of some arbitrary figure is no better than time unit billing. Why not be paid for the true value you bring? If you don't believe that, the client won't either.

Professions that focus on commodity billing—be they legal, financial, architectural, search, consulting, or any other—are those that don't believe their own value proposition in terms of client outcome and, therefore, can't adequately make a case for it.

EDUCATING THE BUYER INCORRECTLY

An inherent problem in the lunacy of time and materials billing is that we educate the client incorrectly from the first meeting. Buyers are willing to believe that we operate in certain ways—just as the client does—and that those methods of operating will somehow have to be accommodated.

Yet we often show up as supplicants and fawners, obsequious in our determination to get the business. We position ourselves as vendors and "salespeople" from the outset, not as credible peers of the buyer.

Hear this: In true client/consultant partnerships, neither party wants to put the other at a disadvantage. Partners simply don't do that to each other. But in superior/subordinate relationships, the superior usually doesn't care, either from callousness, noblesse oblige, or indifference.

Our job is to educate prospects from square zero about how we operate. That means that certain steps are important to take and others important to avoid. Use the following as a checklist to assess your own effectiveness in educating buyers.

Prospect Education Checklist

1. Never quote a fee before project objectives and their value to the client are stipulated. (See Chapter 4, p. 58, for "conceptual agreement.")
2. Don't quote any time unit basis at all.
3. Explain to the client, if pressed, that single, value-based fees are in the client's best interests (see the ethical discussion above).
4. Resist comparison to other consultants by pointing out that the prospect probably also operates differently in many respects from his or her own competitors.
5. Never commit to arbitrary amounts of time for the accomplishment of objectives.

6. Focus on result, not on task.

7. Never accept a prospect's conclusion—stated or implied—that you will constantly be onsite, or that you're available "on call."

8. Emphasize results, not deliverables; in fact, minimize deliverables.

9. Don't accept contingency fees or "pay for performance"; you're not a trained animal act, variables are often outside your control, and besides, you're being paid for your best advice. It's up to the client to implement effectively.

10. Provide value immediately. Shift the focus to how much value you provide, not on how much work there is to be done.

I've found that, in most cases, the consultant creates his or her own quicksand by undermining any possibility of value-based fees at initial meetings, by ignoring or acting contrary to the rules above.

If you explain to the client that you're a performing horse, the client will understandably ask you to jump over hurdles and stand on your hind legs. If you explain that you're a partner interested in helping to generate results, the client will understandably ask, "How do *we* do that best?"

There are two parties concerned about maximizing results—you and the client. But there is only one of you concerned about maximizing your fees. If you emphasize the former, the latter will occur. But if you treat these as two separate considerations with the buyer, that person will try to maximize the former and minimize the latter every time.

Wouldn't you?

- Supply and demand is for commodities, not consultants. Your supply will always exceed demand, and that tells you something about the inherent stupidity of this bromide.
- There are legitimate and obvious ethical reasons not to use time units for billing bases.
- Profitability should not be arbitrarily delimited by finite measures of time, materials, deliverables, and costs.
- Other professions do it incorrectly. Why would you want to emulate them?
- The buyer is educable and you are the teacher. Don't abdicate that huge responsibility.

The average attorney's income is under $100,000 annually. Successful people drive cars that cost more than that. What model are you using as your income paradigm, and what model car are you driving?

The Basics of Value-Based Fees

It's Better to Be an Artist than to Be an Engineer

Clients traditionally are somewhat stunned by and resistant to fees based on anything other than time and materials. That's because we, as consultants, have educated them all wrong. In fact, most consultants are somewhat stunned and resistant to fees based on value, so it's not surprising that the client assumes the same position.

Before we examine the components of the approach that reverses this mentality, let's examine a requisite philosophy: The goal of a consulting intervention is to improve the client's condition by meeting and/or exceeding mutually established project goals. If those goals are thus met or bettered, the resultant improvements will justify any reasonable investment required to achieve that particular return.

Whether quantitatively or qualitatively, whether analytically or viscerally, whether long-term or short-term, we are seeking improvements that dwarf the costs of the consultant. (See Figure 1.3 in the first chapter.) This is both art and science. Part of the art is that the resultant picture has to be enjoyable for the client. Some paintings are very lifelike, some are cubist, some are abstract. But the point is that the client likes the resulting work.

In that case, it doesn't matter whether your fee could have been $15,000 higher or lower, so long as the client is happy and you believe you've been paid fairly and well. Consequently, the point of value-based fees is that both the client and the consultant feel well-treated and are happy with the finished picture. Engineers seek perfection of angles, lines, and support. Artists seek happiness.

FOCUSING ON OUTCOMES NOT ON INPUTS

The very worst failing that consultants possess in relation to fees has nothing to do with fees and everything to do with outcomes. If you accept the fact that the results of a project—the client's improved condition—will determine the acceptable range of investment for that return, then the outcomes for the client are the key determinant in fees.

That's right: It's the outcome, not the tasks, that matter.

> Most consultants place their value proposition at the wrong end of the equation—they focus on their ability to *do* rather than on the client's ability to *improve.*

If you don't believe me, then please accept this challenge. Visit the websites or obtain the printed literature of any five consultants at random. (Or, at an event, engage them in conversation and ask them the reasons for their success.) You will find the following applies to four out of the five, at a minimum:

- *Too many words:* The promotional literature will have far too much text, using a thousand words in place of every possible picture.

- *Self-aggrandizing:* The material will overwhelmingly focus on what the consultant does and how it is done.
- *Technology/methodology smothered:* There will be detailed discussions of the consulting approaches, including analogies, graphs, steps, and jargon.
- *Programmatic orientation:* There will be client "options" in terms of workshops, interventions, materials, and even fee ranges.
- *Value secrecy:* There will be precious little of value to the reader or the listener in terms of immediate improvement.

I can make money by betting on the outcome of this test every time. The problem is that consultants focus on task—what they do—and not on result—what the client gets.

Not only is this a rather unappealing sales proposition (it's nothing more than the "billboard on a highway" approach), but it establishes improper criteria from the very earliest prospect interactions. If that prospect becomes a client, he or she has been inculcated—by us—to appreciate our value as based on what we do and how often we do it. In other words, it's the brush strokes, the framing, and the colors used in creating the painting, rather than the overall aesthetic power of the finished picture.

Every intervention and activity you propose to the client must be cast as an outcome and result. The intrinsic value of the former is minor. Tasks are basically commodities that can be compared and contrasted. The intrinsic value of the latter is enormous, because they meet client emotional and visceral needs, and they can't be compared to anything else. *The exclusive difference in the client's perception of "task" and commodity or "result" and outcome is within your power to influence.* Most of us have abdicated the responsibility.

On the list below, the first statement is a task, followed by a statement in italics, which represents a possible outcome:

- Conduct focus groups throughout the sales division. *Determine the causes for turnover among top sales talent.*
- Coach the senior vice president of finance. *Enable the CFO to become a full partner in the executive team during a time of acquisitions and mergers in this company.*
- Clarify understanding of strategy during a retreat and gain senior management consensus on direction. *Establish a new and aggressive strategy for*

the next two years, which will fulfill the board's desire for double-digit revenue growth and 10 percent gain in market share.

- Analyze the feasibility of a purchase of the competitor's Acme Division. *Maximize the return on the prospective $2 billion Acme acquisition, or protect the company from making a bad investment.*

Most of us think in terms of what we do, not in terms of how the client will act. It's insane to base fees on things that are important to us instead of on what's important to the client.

This slight change of emphasis from our help to the client's outcome is simple to accomplish, yet is the main ingredient in preparing the client for value-based pricing. Our job is to establish the client's improvement, not to harp on the efficacy of our approaches (which aren't really efficacious, anyway, unless the client sees improvement). I love the consultants who claim, "My recommendations were excellent, based on outstanding focus group work. Your managers just aren't using the findings to gain the needed changes." I've got news for you: If the changes aren't forthcoming, then the project has failed, irrespective of the focus groups and the recommendations.

PRACTICUM

Even ultimate consultants can have homework. Go through every piece of your promotional material, every page of your website, every remark you tend to make in speeches or casual conversation about your work, and ask whether it meets the client results test: Do the remarks and text focus on client improvement and results, or do they focus on your actions and your methods? Change everything—100 percent—to the former. It's far better to have a prospect say, "I'm not sure how you work to get these results. Can you explain it to me?" than it is to have one say, "I'm not sure how I benefit from what you do."

Move the prospect from what you do to how the prospect benefits as early as possible in the contact and/or discussions. Ultimately, your fees will be based on those early moments.

THE FALLACY AND SUBVERSIVE NATURE OF "DELIVERABLES"

Because consultants tend to place little value on their advice and counsel (which is a low self-esteem issue), they have to find some device or technique in which to vest their value. That alternative is usually the dreaded "D" word: deliverables.

I've seen proposals that feature deliverables as the key aspect of the entire consulting engagement.[1] Imagine: A report, manual, class, set of recommendations, or even presentation to management becomes the signal aspect of the consultant's contribution to results. There's a reason that a school teacher makes $40,000 for a year's work, and Colin Powell, prior to his government job, made $75,000 for a forty-five-minute keynote speech. Teachers are not evaluated on results (student admission to college, acquisition of good jobs, scores on standardized tests, etc.), and, in fact, have fought against it. Former General Powell was evaluated on the results of his appearance for employees, customers, management, leadership, morale, and so on. As long as both are positioned as they are, both deserve what they get. (No one would pay $75,000 for forty-five minutes, and no one would pay only $40,000 for his or her child's future. This is why so few of us stand out in a crowd.)

A deliverable is a means to an end. It is a progress point or way station along the way to client results. But deliverables themselves are not client results, and they should never be emphasized or confused in that regard.

---

[1]See my book, *How to Write a Proposal That's Accepted Every Time* (Kennedy Information, 1999), for a format that avoids deliverables completely.

> There is no reason on earth that a consulting project can't be sold, implemented successfully, and concluded brilliantly without a single mention of "deliverables." Unless, of course, that's what the consultant is selling, implementing, and concluding.

The key in avoiding deliverables is not to talk about them, but to talk about value and outcomes instead. Don't underestimate the importance of the self-esteem factor, because other consultants have probably educated the buyer incorrectly, and the buyer might be using deliverables as a favorite criterion to assess consulting proposals.

It's fair to give your prospect a notion of the type of methodology you'll be using. For example, focus groups require active client participation, while interviews by phone with clients require practically none. Classroom training requires scheduling, while job performance aids do not. Observation of the client environment and conditions creates a "Hawthorne effect" (an awareness and behavior change on the part of those being observed), while "shopping the customer's business" incognito does not. However, providing numbers of programs, exact participation, reports stipulated at given junctures, and appearances at meetings is more than the client needs to know.

You are the consulting expert. You've been contacted, presumably, because the client needs help that is not available internally and hasn't thus far been secured externally. If the client were adept at consulting—or even at improving the desired condition—you wouldn't be involved in the conversation. The prospect needs help not currently accessible.

Don't sacrifice that potential power base by acceding to client demands that are arbitrary, anxious, and often amateurish. The answer to "How many reports will you provide and how often?" is not "How many do you want and how frequently?" or "How about twice a month?" The answer is, "Who cares? The reports aren't the point. Improvement in your retention rate is the point, and we'll all know that when we see it."

I was contacted by Mercedes-Benz North America, which has an incredibly stringent method of choosing consultants. First, they sent a delegation to hear me speak at a client event. Second, they invited me in to meet with another level of evaluators. Third, they placed the few of us who survived in front of the buyer.

The buyer, a tough authoritarian figure from the German parent, told me how the consulting project would be conducted, asked me how I would conform to those specifications, and wanted a precise schedule of deliverables. He also demanded to know the precise depth of my auto expertise and what I intended to do prior to the engagement to strengthen it.

I told him that I didn't operate that way and it wouldn't help him, either, even if I did.

He was aghast. (His subordinates ducked for cover.) I told him, as I gestured around the room, that he was surrounded by auto experts, and the last thing he needed was another one from the outside. Mercedes knew how to make cars. I wasn't going to tell them how to improve their fuel injection or brake linings. But I knew how to consult, and I wasn't about to let Mercedes tell me how to gather data or validate my findings. The partnership was based on what we both were good at, or there was no synergy and no partnership.

I got the job, and the fee was never discussed until my proposal was signed. The buyer, since retired, told me much later on a plane trip that he wished his subordinates had the courage of their convictions to speak to him the way I had.

In fact, we may decide, as the consulting experts, to change, add, or delete deliverables as the project progresses, so it's folly to base our value on the types and volume of them. If I brief a client by phone, a written report may no longer be necessary. If five focus groups turn up an absolutely valid pattern, then the other five may be dispensed with (and if all ten are inconclusive, you might have to do another ten). I've seen "deliverables" from consultants that were superfluous, redundant, simplistic, and superficial. But they were "delivered" nonetheless, because the consultant and client both believed that they were what the client was paying for.

A final word on deliverables to purposely belabor the obvious. The absolute worst deliverable to suggest, commit to, and base fees on is your TIME. When your value is based on showing up, you tend to show up, whether you're needed or not. When the client expects to see you, the client looks for you, whether it makes sense for you to be there or not. I've seen proposals that quoted as a deliverable "fourteen days on site over two months," or "visits to every site twice a month," or "participation in every weekly executive committee meeting."

If your fees are based on deliverables, and your primary deliverable is your time, you might as well become a plumber or electrician. They are booked more often than you, have clear and finite projects, and seldom require a plane trip to fix a sink or repair an outlet.

I've conducted projects for Hewlett-Packard, one of the greatest and smartest organizations on the planet, during which I never showed up once. That's right; everything took place by phone, fax, email, research, teleconference, and other remote means. They have been ecstatic with the results. I've been ecstatic with the fees. No one has asked why they haven't seen me lately. Part of the key is that HP is truly a global company, with key people at every level of management located all over the world. They don't expect to see each other, and they don't expect to see me.

You need to get into an "HP frame of mind."

QUANTITATIVE AND QUALITATIVE MEASURES AND CRITERIA

Fees that are based on true outcomes and client results require that some metrics be established for those results so that you and the client can relate the improved client condition to your involvement, and not the fates or the actions of others. (One thing about "deliverables" is that the client knows them when you've "delivered" them, but that's hardly justification for basing fees on them.)

There are two kinds of metrics to assign to the desired client outcomes: quantitative (improvement by an objective yardstick) and qualitative (improvement by an agreed on subjective reference point).

Quantitative or Objective Criteria

The objective measures of client improvement are clear and obvious. They include areas such as:

- market share
- profits
- customer ratings
- return on investment
- return on equity
- retention of clients
- numbers of new sales
- product to market time
- revenues
- response time
- employee ratings
- return on sales
- return on assets
- retention of employees
- margin per sale
- installed systems

The list could go on and on. However, there are several critical aspects to even such clear and objective measures.

First, the nature of the measurement device must be agreed on. Will it be the monthly sales reports, the sales call sheets, the finance department's weekly profit report, or the six-month review of retained business? In many cases, clients will think they are measuring objective data, but they are really relying on anecdotal reports from subjective sources. (Sales managers are notorious for this.) It's up to the consultant to evaluate the metric and help the client establish a sound one if none exists or if the current ones are inadequate. By assisting in the evaluation and possible development of metrics, you are immediately adding value to the project, which should be reflected in your fee. (*That's right:* Establishing the criteria for your own project's success justifies a higher fee.)

> The direction of the result is far better—and safer—than the specification of the exact result. There are too many variables involved for you to rely on the attainment of a "magic number."

Second, you cannot base your contribution on what I call a "magic number." While a 6 percent increase in sales might be highly desirable and even, in your opinion, very achievable, it's never a good idea to peg your success to that magic number. The reason is that there are far too many variables that can affect that number adversely for you to take that risk. For example, if three top sales people are recruited away by a competitor's unmatchable offer, or a new technology undermines the client's older technology, or three key client customers suffer setbacks affecting the client's business, you can hardly be held accountable.

It's better to state that you will assist in maximizing the sales increase, or drive attrition down to industry averages, or increase profit-per-sale, or decrease costs of acquisition. But tying yourself to a "magic number" is fraught with danger.

I know what you're thinking: But what if the outcomes are far in excess of an agreed on number? Can't I take a piece of that greater result? If it's just "progress toward," then I'm cheating myself.

This is contingency fee theory, and the lawyers love it. But I'd warn you about this: Excessive results are probably not going to be attributed to you anyway, since the client will tend to say, "We're doing so well we probably didn't need you after all." Second, the client will tend to be resentful at paying you more and more as results climb and climb. Third, this dynamic means that you'll have to reduce your fee if you fail to hit the magic mark (fair is fair). Finally, your own consulting judgment will be clouded by the conflict of true, long-term progress versus short-term growth and your mercenary stake in it.

You're better off taking a single, flat fee with a very high margin and counting on future business if the client is hugely successful. You're almost guaranteed to get it under these circumstances.

Qualitative or Subjective Criteria

In some of my most successful projects, the criteria for success were subjective, although of very high quality, nonetheless. By "high quality," I mean that different outcomes represent very different levels of satisfaction. The beauty of a building, the public repute of a firm, the comfort of office furniture are all examples of rather subjective yet high quality outcomes. An unaesthetic building, a lousy reputation, and uncomfortable seating are all major problems, despite the subjectivity of one's measure.

The key, of course, is: Do we agree on who is doing the measuring and what standards they are applying?

I don't get involved in aesthetics or furniture comfort, but I do take on image, repute, stress, teamwork, communications, and a host of related issues that aren't very conducive to quantitative measures. (The "experts" who claim that, "If you can't measure it, it isn't important" are simply spouting another bromide and are almost always academics or human resource people.) Recently, an organization no less august than the Harvard School of Law undertook a major project with McKinsey & Co. to create a better feeling about the school among its graduates after surveys disclosed that students felt their education was excellent, but that the Harvard Law experience was rather dreadful. Firms such as Andersen were also in on the bidding, which ran into very significant numbers.

> Qualitative measures can be among the most powerful and create the highest fees IF a significant buyer is doing the measuring.

"I'll know it when I see it" may be a sufficient criterion for some members of the Supreme Court to evaluate pornography, but it is insufficient for a consulting project. In fact, here are the parameters for creating a successful, anecdotal series of measures for a project:

- The buyer himself or herself will judge the result
- The effectiveness will rely on observed behavior and factual evidence

- There will be gradations of success, not success or failure (a rheostat, not an "on and off" switch)
- There must be reasonable time limits

MEASURING THE UNMEASURABLE

An example: A CEO of a $600 million operation told me that his objective was to create better teamwork among his direct reports. His own total compensation package was about $2 million. I asked him why (the value) he wanted to do this, and he told me that improved teamwork would:

- Free him up from petty turf issues
- Allow him to focus on the board's requirements for expansion
- Evaluate which subordinates were possible successors
- Speed cross-functional collaboration (since subordinates erected the turf boundaries that their bosses designed)
- Reduce the high frequency and long duration of meetings that were necessary to sort out all the conflict

This was obviously a high value project. But how would we know that we had achieved something. "I'll know it when I see it, believe me," he said, but I didn't believe him. "How would you prove this to the board," I asked, "or to a newspaper reporter doing a story on how much you and I have improved teamwork?"

We arrived at the following measures, which he and I would agree were present or not through observation and participation, which would improve by degrees, and which would require about six months for complete effect:

- Meetings would reduce in frequency and duration, and agenda items would contain fewer and fewer issues to be resolved among departments
- Customers would cease complaining that they were receiving conflicting advice, duplicate bills, and too many sales calls from different people
- Talent would be transferred across departmental lines for succession planning and career development without human resources demanding impasses be broken by the CEO

- Cross-functional collaboration and knowledge sharing would decline from the top spot in the annual employee survey of "most needed" improvements
- The CEO would receive fewer and fewer phone calls and private visits from direct reports demanding that he intercede with their peers

We applied these measures at our own semi-monthly meetings, judged our progress, and made plans for next steps. The project was a great success. The keys for all of us, when dealing with subjective and anecdotal measures, is to agree on the specific behaviors and evidence with the buyer and to compare notes on relative progress frequently.

Qualitative and subjective measures are often the most valuable that a buyer wants to pursue, so don't demand that they be somehow metamorphosed into quantitative metrics and numbers.

SERVING THE CLIENT'S SELF-INTEREST

Value-based fees are most directly related to the client's self-interest being served. That self-interest may be organizational—higher sales, better retention, improved image—or personal—less stress, better time use, improved effectiveness. In either case, it's the buyer who counts.

> People will only change behavior for the long term—that is, with commitment and not just compliance—if their rational self-interest is met. Motivation is intrinsic, and people can only motivate themselves to change.

Prospects will often tell you what they want, but they won't often articulate what they really *need*. That's because they often don't know. They will want an obvious solution or alternative because they haven't been in a position or had the advice to view the situation more dispassionately and objectively, or haven't had the frame of reference or innovative ability to create a better response.

That's why they need you or me. It's the height of folly to sacrifice that need by dutifully and mindlessly (and valuelessly) complying with the buyer's stated "wants." After all the work and intelligence required to reach a true buyer, it's worse than negligent to simply reply to that person's desires without examining them for deeper and more important needs.

The key question at this juncture is a simple one: "Why?" Why does the buyer want a sales training program? If more sales are required to compensate for client turnover, maybe the real need is better customer service. If the buyer wants coaching to improve delegation skills, maybe the real need is to change a culture that is authoritarian and rejects empowerment and delegation. If the client wants a mentoring program to improve retention of new employees, maybe the selection process is using incorrect criteria or the competition uses better non-financial incentives to lure people away.

All clients know what they want. Few know what they need. It's imperative to explore this early and tap into the buyer's self-interest, which is always going to be to find the best organizational and/or personal improvement. If that improvement is more than they had envisioned, all the better, and your method for obtaining it and compensation for your method are small potatoes indeed.

Many consultants attempt to enlarge sales (especially those based on a time-and-materials billing system) by "enlarging" them to include more areas, more people, or longer durations. This is madness, since it also increases the labor intensity of the project, which is arithmetic growth at best.

The key to geometric growth is to find that rich vein of true need and mine it assiduously. When the buyer says, "We've never looked at it that way before," or "Why, that's counter-intuitive," or "I've never considered that, and I can't imagine why not," you've achieved a wonderful sale, which you can only louse up if you don't understand where you are.

This is why promoting how good you are; touting your methodology; demonstrating patents, copyrights, and trademarks; and attempting to dazzle the prospect with the beauty of your intricate approaches are all so silly. None of that is in the prospect's self-interest. But I can sit down without one sheet of paper and without, thank the fates, any reference at all to PowerPoint, and demonstrate how the buyer will be much better off as a result of our partnership, including in those areas where the buyer hadn't even been aware of the opportunities.

That beats a slide show any day.

> No one cares, really, about how good you are. They care about how good they are going to be when you're done with them.

THE SUBTLE TRANSFORMATION: CONSULTANT PAST TO CLIENT FUTURE

The final major consideration to think about—or, perhaps, to internalize—is that we, as consultants, are engaged in a rather grand venture. We are not worth our appearances, we are not worth our technology, we are not worth our tactical advice. Of course, you can charge for all that, but your fees will be delimited by the very nature of the limitations of those components.

We are actually worth the transformation that we achieve in turning our history into the client's future. Figure 3.1 shows the actual process flow that all of us should bear in mind with every project.

All of us possess a unique background that we should accentuate, not blend into a homogeneous consultant "hash." The longer we work, and the

Consultant's Past	Current Intervention	Client's Future
• experiences	• coaching	• higher productivity
• education	• survey	• lower attrition
• accomplishments	• redesign	• higher morale
• development	• workshop	• improved image
• travels	• retreat	• better performance
• work history	• etc.	• greater market share
• beliefs		• greater profit
• victories/defeats		• more growth
• risks/adversity		• more innovation
• experimentation		• problems solved
		• happier customers
		• superior service

Process Flow
⟶

Figure 3.1. Transforming Consultant Past to Client Future

more diverse our projects, the richer that background. (This is also why I preach that academic degrees are only a small part of one's armamentarium.) We transfer that *past* to the client through a series of *interventions,* which might include major interactive devices (training, focus groups), personalized interaction (coaching, interviews), proprietary approaches (books, models), and individual work (observations, advice).

The mistake is to attach a value and a fee to either of the first two columns. The only column that matters is the third column: the client results, which, of course, constitute the client's *future.*

Yet even the best of consultants, while acknowledging project objectives and outcomes, retrogress and assess their fees based on the number of retreats, or the size of a survey, or their history in that industry, or how many sites they'll have to visit. The worst consultants never visit the third column at all.

I invite you to use Figure 3.1 as a template.[2] The left column generic headings should be replaced by your own unique past, and that column should grow continually. (If it's not growing after every single engagement, then you're taking on projects you can do blindfolded and you're not growing and, thus, not increasing your potential value.) The middle column should be your particular interventions, and they might be stable or grow (or even decline). For example, you may add "expert witness" to that column. I, for one, have deleted "training" from that column, which I choose not to do any more. Generally, since we have a limited range of competencies and tend to focus on what we do best, this column will be relatively shorter than the others.

The ability to use a selected variety of interventions to interpret our past for the client's improved future is a rare dynamic, one shared, perhaps, with doctors and lawyers. But the doctors seldom have our range of possible work, and the lawyers have no idea how to charge for their value. That leaves the field to us.

---

[2]The form first appeared in the first book of this series, *The Ultimate Consultant* (Jossey-Bass/Pfeiffer, 2001), and I hope you'll read that work if you haven't already.

The third column we should generate for each particular client. It should be as long as possible and be created with the buyer's active collaboration and contributions (thus stipulating to the value we're providing). Yet, overwhelmingly, our approaches, promotional material, conversations, and even ideas about self-worth tend to focus on the first two columns and not the third. As Marshal Ney said when told of the assassination of a rival ordered by Napoleon, "It's worse than a crime. It's a blunder."

PERPETUAL MOTION = PERPETUAL PROGRESS

There is nothing magic, or even new, about my models. Substitute them for others of your own design if you like. But the point not to be lost is that you must have a conscious model for determining your value to the client, and your models, whatever they are, must start with your own acceptance and buy-in. The first sale is always to yourself.

Never view the client as a fixed position moving to another fixed position. I'm told that the best airplane pilots are able to immediately visualize movements in three dimensions, since an airplane, even when taking off, is not moving merely forward or up, but is moving in several directions at once whenever airborne. Similarly, a client doesn't merely move from position "A" to position "B," but rather moves dynamically, somewhat to the left or right, a little up or down. Client success is a moving target, which should always be a goal, not a destination.

Therefore, our ability to impact the client's future is an ongoing need and a continual value. If we're really good, the collaboration isn't just about reaching point "B," it's about continually describing and preparing for new futures and the requisite journeys.

And as you accompany the client on that journey, you are constantly learning and increasing the fuel in the first column, enabling the third column to continually be enriched. That's right: The very work you do with a client should make you more valuable to that client as time progresses. One of the bromides in this business is that a consultant comes to study a problem and remains to become part of it. I don't doubt that many do just that. But the flip side of the value coin is that, once you're working in partnership with the buyer to enrich the future, and you're constantly learning during the process—thereby further increasing your value—why would a client want you to leave?

Don't misunderstand. I'm not advocating clients-for-life, or some kind of viral approach where the client is never free of you. But I am maintaining that we come and go too quickly, in general, and that we underestimate the improving value we provide *simply by dint of successfully working with the client and reaching our joint goals in real time.* We leave too early because we disengage too early, and we disengage too early because we don't think it's "right" to market while we deliver.

This is crazy. It's perfectly fine to continue to improve our own value while providing the client with increasing value as a result. I worked with Merck for twelve years in a row; with Calgon for five; and with Hewlett-Packard for over fifteen. There were and are some very smart people there. I'd like to think they recognized a good thing—a high value—when they saw it.

This is the "good deal" to which I periodically refer: When a buyer says, "He was a bargain," and I say, "I was well-paid," that's the basis for continued high value and ongoing high profits—for both parties.

The opportunity to turn our past into the client's future is very existential. Our past improves as our work with the client progresses. As that value grows, so should our client relationship and the duration of our partnership.

CHAPTER 3 ROI

- The basis for value-based fees is in client results, not consultant tasks. We tend to focus on the wrong side of that equation.
- "Deliverables" are a consultant-invented shibboleth that is easier to describe and produce than ultimate value. They are also of far less worth.
- Measures of success can be quantitative and qualitative, and the latter—with the subjective assessment of the buyer—can be more valuable than the former.
- Buyer self-interest—either organizational or individual—is the key. Consultant self-interest is merely a function of the buyer's needs.

- What a buyer wants and what a buyer needs are two different things in most cases, and it's up to the consultant to demonstrate the difference and the greater value of that difference.
- We transform our unique past into the client's unique future. When stated (and believed) in that framework, it's difficult to place a high enough fee on that tremendous value.

Consulting is art and science. The danger is that we become excellent technicians and lose our aesthetic sense. We need to paint visions of the future—for our clients and for ourselves.

How to Establish Value-Based Fees

If You Read Only One Chapter . . .

Ever since I began promoting value-based pricing for consultants (and the variety of other occupations and professions that have sought to heed the call), I've been asked one question consistently by a minority of the acolytes: "What formula should I use?"

That, of course, is the million-dollar question. Fee setting is art and science, and mostly the former. Consequently, the engineers, architects, and other highly structured among us have had to be revived when told that there is no magic formula. However, that's not to say that there aren't excellent ways to create fees based on value, if you're willing to be flexible, confident, and diagnostic.

So if you haven't rushed to get your money back after the first two paragraphs, I can be of considerable help. In fact, for the first time I'm going to be very explicit in writing about the creation of value-based fees. But please keep these precepts in mind:

- The idea is to create high *margins,* not merely high fees. That way, you can afford to be less precise about fees, since the margins will allow for plenty of flexibility.
- Value is in the eye of the beholder. There is no law, nor any ethical imperative, that says that you must charge two clients the exact same amount for the same services. First, the services are rarely identical. Second, the value to those respective clients will always be different.
- The fact that you could do something for less money, or that you could do more for the same amount of money, is irrelevant. The only relevant facts are: Are you meeting the client's objectives, improving the client's condition, and delighting your buyer? You virtually never have to provide every single service, every scintilla of information, or every day of your life to do that.

CONCEPTUAL AGREEMENT: THE FOUNDATION OF VALUE

This is a relationship business. Trust is essential to relationships. When a buyer trusts you—and you trust the buyer—you are in a position to acquire the three essential building blocks for a value-based project:

1. The business objectives to be met
2. The metrics or measures of success to assess progress
3. The value to the client of meeting those objectives

A relationship with an economic buyer is ALWAYS the first step in a value-based project. You don't need anyone else, but you can't make the sale with anyone else either. It's that simple.

That's it. That's all you need from the client to create a fee based on value. And you can only obtain that from the economic buyer. The sequence here is simple and straightforward, but also ineffable (see Figure 4.1).

As you can see in Figure 4.1, our marketing efforts create leads, which we pursue and qualify to find the true (economic) buyer—the person who can write a check for our services. We then establish a relationship with that buyer so that we can gain conceptual agreement about the three criteria above. Without the economic buyer, the discussion is irrelevant; without a trusting relationship, the important information is unlikely to be shared; and without conceptual agreement, we are unable to establish the value *as perceived by the client,* which is the key input to our own fees.

One last time, then:

- *Objectives:* Those business outcomes (for example, higher sales, better teamwork, faster time to market) that are essential for the project to deliver for the client
- *Measures:* Those objective or subjective (anecdotal) criteria that will indicate progress and, eventually, completion for client and consultant
- *Value:* The demonstrable benefit, organizational and/or personal, stipulated by the client as representing the actual improvement in the client's condition

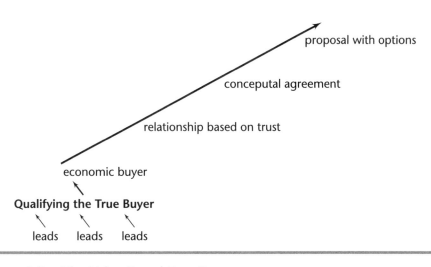

Figure 4.1. The Value-Based Fees Sequence

Setting value-based fees is both art and science. But a key criterion is simply this: What fee range is likely to prompt the client to say, "That was a terrific return on my investment, and I'd like to work with that person again," and you to say, "I was paid very well for my contribution, and the margin was excellent."

I'll provide some "formulas" for this at the end of this chapter, but it's imperative that you understand the underlying rationale first. The economic buyer must agree to outcomes, measures, and value of the improvements in collaboration with you prior to setting fees. If you accomplish this, your proposals will be accepted over 80 percent of the time (although you'll probably submit fewer proposals than you do now). If you ignore this, your chances of having value-based proposals accepted are less than 5 percent.

Here's an example for our purposes:

Project

- Improve retention of new employees in a zero-unemployment, highly competitive environment

Objectives

- Current rate of new employee turnover (32 percent) lowered toward industry average (22 percent) over one year's time
- Hiring process improved so that fewer poor candidates "survive" to third round of interviews
- Causes for high turnover understood and patterns traced to relevant sources: interviews, orientation, training, mentor, supervisor, etc.

Measures

- Monthly retention report and turnover statistics
- Exit interview analysis

- Survey (to be created) for new hires to accept and reject company offer letter
- Six, twelve, and eighteen-month "survivor" rates

Value

- Current turnover costing $545,000 annually in actual salary, benefits, and related expenses
- Estimated cost of lost work, poor productivity, overtime, and related costs until vacated jobs are ultimately filled by qualified and trained replacements: $2,600,000 annually
- Estimated cost of "failure work" in senior management interviewing candidates who should have been eliminated at lower levels: $350,000 annually

In my basic example, this client is spending about $3,500,000 on an inadequate and ineffective hiring process. And that's just annually. We'll return to this example once we establish a few more basics. But note that the economic buyer has provided these numbers in discussions with the consultant.[1]

ESTABLISHING YOUR UNIQUE VALUE

The work above helps to establish value in terms of buyer needs. A second major component of value, however, can be ascertained without the buyer's involvement, and that's your uniqueness and personal contribution.

There are three questions that you should answer in every single engagement, prior to establishing fees:

1. Why me?
2. Why now?
3. Why in this manner?

---

[1]See Appendices A through F for examples of the questions that can be used with the economic buyer to establish objectives, measures, value, etc.

Why Me?

If there are hundreds of consultants who can do the work in question and provide the value that the client requests, then you are less valuable to the success of this project. But if the number of consultants who can do the work is limited, then your value increases. This is basic supply-and-demand mentality, but in this limited question, it works.

Here are some components of this question that can help you determine whether you are uniquely valuable or simply another fish in the school:

- Is the buyer talking to other consultants (and, if so, a limited range or a great many)?
- Do you possess some unique expertise or history (you "wrote the book," once worked in the industry, worked for the buyer in the past, etc.)?
- Have you been referred to the buyer by a trusted source?
- Are you known within the industry, or do you have a unique reputation?
- Are you at the right place at the right time (you're local, you're available to start immediately, etc.)?

Ask yourself whether you bring some inherent value that others can't, whether by design (a book you've written) or by accident (you're the only one who can begin next week). Sometimes it's as important to be lucky as it is to be good.

It's easy to assess your own unique value, but most consultants don't bother. If you don't do it, no one else is going to do it for you.

Why Now?

Is there some special value about this juncture that needs to be factored in? After all, there is often a reason why the discussion is being undertaken today and not six months ago or six months from now, and that reason is often desperation!

Some component questions:

- What if the client did nothing? Would the situation be stable or deteriorate still further?
- Is there a limited window of opportunity during which gains must be made or they will be lost?
- Has something occurred that has increased the urgency significantly (for example, the CEO has said, "Get it done!")?
- Are certain conditions in place that need to be capitalized on or they will be lost (for example, a competitor's temporary misfortune)?
- Is there funding available that will disappear if not used (often the case at the conclusion of a fiscal year)?

When a prospect contacts you, there is always an implied urgency. The key is to determine just how great it is, or to increase it through your relationship with the buyer.

Why in This Manner?

Hiring a consultant is hardly a default position, as much as we would all wish it were. There must be reasons mitigating in favor of such a hire if the buyer is bothering to talk to you (irrespective of whether the buyer reached out to you or you to the buyer).[2]

Additional questions:

- Why aren't they doing this internally?
- Have they tried this in the past and failed?
- Have they used other consultants in the past and, if so, with what result?
- Why is this buyer the one who is the sponsor of this project?
- Who else is involved in this project and why?

By determining special circumstances, you'll be in a position to establish your ability to contribute to those special needs.

---

[2]I want to emphasize that my remarks pertain to true buyers. Gatekeepers, trainers, human resource people, purchasing agents, and others will often reach out simply to "shop" and compare prices. These approaches are not designed for such contacts. The only thing to do with those contacts is to use them to reach an economic buyer.

In establishing your own unique value, you have another important input to your fee determination. (Note that many of the questions in these three areas may be answered in your relationship building with the buyer. Keep them in mind—even written in your notes—as your discussion progresses.)

> Almost any time a client contacts you, there is the strong possibility that an urgency, need, and responsiveness exist that are greater than initially indicated. This is why effective marketing is so important: Prospects contacting you are much more inherently valuable than prospects you contact. The entire value proposition is different.

At this point, you have two excellent sources or indicators of the contribution you are providing to the client's improvement:

1. The stipulated value that the successful completion of the project will deliver to the client
2. The unique qualities that you, personally, bring to the equation to ensure that those results are met and exceeded

It's now time to appreciate the extent of this mutual "good deal."

CREATING THE "GOOD DEAL" DYNAMIC

Customers buy cheap pens and expensive cars for the same reason: The purchase makes sense in terms of what they care to invest at that moment. The pen may be easily lost on the job and is used only for internal signoffs on inventory, so the quality doesn't matter as long as the loss isn't too great when the pen inevitably disappears. In that case, 19 cents makes sense.

The car may cost $75,000, but there are few like it, you feel good in it, and you've always wanted one. You can now afford it. The emotional gratification more than compensates for the difference in the basic cost of auto transportation that could be saved with a less expensive vehicle.

In either case, it's a "good deal" for the customer. You have to make a "good deal" for the buyer. Note that this is more than merely a return on investment. That's because good deals are based on visceral and subjective needs as much as on analytic and objective needs (which is why you always want to stay away from the obsessively detailed denizens of the purchasing department). Focus on these "good deal" factors while building your relationship and establishing conceptual agreement (and find out which are most crucial to your buyer):

- Responsiveness (a plus for solo practitioners)
- Referral source (the transferred trust from the person referring you)
- Speed of completion
- Transfer of skills so that the client can replicate
- Using an "authority" or acknowledged "expert"
- Documentation
- Involvement of client personnel
- Confidentiality, non-disclosure, and/or non-compete
- Use and/or transfer or proprietary material
- Guarantees and assurances
- Industry knowledge or experience[3]
- Accountability for tough decisions (you are the "black hat")
- Ability to travel and visit sites
- Technological compatibility
- Safety (malpractice insurance, liability insurance, etc.)[4]

Not all of these issues will apply. But you won't know unless you check for them. Also, you'll note that "fees" or "costs" are never mentioned as part of the "good deal" evaluation. That's because the good deal is based on *value* and not on fees. At no point are we attempting to establish a good deal on the basis of

---

[3]While I'm not an advocate of industry specialization, if you just happen to have worked in the field, you probably have an advantage if you position it correctly.

[4]A consultant cannot work for Hewlett-Packard without evidence of an in-force malpractice insurance policy, for example.

lower price, because *a good deal must benefit both parties, and lower fees do not benefit the consultant.* Hence, fees should not be a part of this list.

> Assess those emotional and psychological factors that may prompt a buyer to perceive that he or she is getting a really good deal. That same process will enable you to raise fees, provided that the "good deal" is not about lowering fees!

The "good deal" equation for the buyer can include any or all of these variables:

- *Duration:* The benefits of the project are annualized and forever, while the fee is one time and fixed
- *Skills Transfer:* The client's people will be able to do this themselves in the future, not only solving the immediate problem, but creating an internal capability for future problems
- *Leading Edge:* The client will be assuming a leading-edge position in the industry, marketplace, community, or whatever the environment; above and beyond the issue, the perception and image impact are substantial
- *Control of One's Destiny:* Just by dint of doing something—hiring you—the client has extricated the organization from the morass; almost any action can have a positive effect,[5] even if results aren't quickly appreciated

Ultimately, the equation might look like Figure 4.2.

---

[5]The classic case being the near-legendary "Hawthorne studies," which showed that raising the lighting positively affected performance, but so did lowering the lighting. It was the attention, not the actual light setting, that mattered in terms of productivity.

An attorney at one of the largest consulting firms in the world told me that he was an advocate of value-based fees. His problem was that his accounting department forced him to report the fee on some kind of hourly basis, so that the result—say $2,500 per hour—was intolerable to even the most liberal and understanding client.

A client, who didn't mind paying $60,000 for the value of the attorney's consulting, nearly choked when the attorney's own firm positioned it as a huge amount per hour, since they would only bill for actual time spent and not value delivered to the client.

The attorney asked my advice for how to handle the client. I told him not to handle the client, but to handle his own operation. He had to go to his own CEO and explain that he could either lower his overall fee generation for the consulting firm by about 80 percent or that the CEO could pressure accounting into changing its procedures for recording revenues. Did they want the current Jurassic bookkeeping and $250,000 of revenue or a value-based system and over $1 million?

Accounting quickly found another way to report income. There's no excuse for this, even in large, bureaucratic firms, and certainly none whatsoever in small firms or solo practices.

The key is: Don't seek to lower the divisor by lowering fees; seek to increase the dividend (the benefits and peripherals) so that the quotient—the good deal—is maximized.

$$\frac{\text{Tangible Outcomes X Expected Duration of Outcomes +}}{\text{Intangible Outcomes X Emotional Impact of Intangibles +}}_{\text{Peripheral Benefits + Variables Positively Affected}} = \text{Client's "Good Deal"}$$

Figure 4.2. The "Good Deal" Equation

THE INCREDIBLY POWERFUL "CHOICE OF YESES"

No client should ever have to make a "go/no go" decision, yet that is exactly the narrow box that most consultants force on their buyers.

The psychological shift from "Should I use Alan?" to "*How* should I use Alan?" is enormous. The buyer, in the latter instance, actually enters into a collaboration with you to determine how best to apply your talents and use your contribution. The former, a binary choice, is a sales proposition; the latter, a pluralistic choice, is a partnership proposition.

> By simply providing options, you move the sale to an assumptive close, and the fees to a "migratory range" which is ever upward. Every buyer wants to lower fees, but not one wants to lower value.

Another powerful effect of options *is that they relentlessly drive fees upward.* When confronted with three options, each one promising higher value for the client, the buyer will tend to move at least to the second and often to the third. This can't happen with a "take it or leave it" proposal. Buyers may seek to lower fees, but they also seek to maximize value.

Here is a brief example of options used in a project involving gathering employee feedback on desirable benefits to retain talent.

Option #1. We will conduct focus groups throughout the company, representing about 15 percent of the population. The value of these includes "self-sanctioning" groups, which will separate a "one-off" opinion from the prevailing opinions, and also allow for follow-up and causal questions.

Option #2. We will also provide one-on-one interviews with about 5 percent of the population. This provides the opportunity to bolster the focus groups with confidential opinions, drawn at random, where the individual is not exposed to a larger group. People are often more candid in this situation, particularly those who are relatively unassertive in groups.

Option #3.   We will provide a paper-and-pencil or Internet survey for all members of the population. This will bolster the other options, providing every single employee the opportunity to provide feedback on a confidential and anonymous basis. Note that similar patterns that emerge from the three diverse avenues will be highly valid and most reliable.

Option #4.   We will compare the results of whatever options you choose to benchmark studies we have conducted for other organizations, which will also give you a relative insight into your employee desires and complaints compared to a wider, general population.

Option #5.   We will provide a series of workshops for your key managers in how to deal with, react to, discuss, and take action on the results of the above studies. It's imperative that you have a plan in place to respond rapidly and accurately, but without committing yourself to inappropriate solutions.

In the example above, the first option (based on the overall value of the project to employee retention) might be priced at $45,000; the second at $65,000 (includes the first); the third at $95,000 (includes the first and second); and the fourth at an additional $35,000, despite which of the first three are chosen. Similarly, the fifth might be an additional $45,000. The buyer is in a position to determine whether to take the "risk" of a single avenue of feedback (which, if only one, you determine is best as a focus group) or whether to minimize that risk with other options, including preparing the management team for how to deal with that feedback (Option #5). The decision as to whether to provide for management team training to accompany, say, Option #2, is a far cry from deciding about whether to proceed or not.

Such is the power of options. They can be used at any point in the sale (for example, "We can have a conference call this afternoon, I can call you alone tomorrow, or I can visit you on Monday—which is preferable?"), but are especially key in the proposal when providing for a basis for fees.

Once you've established a general fee range for your contribution based on the value generated (all the factors discussed previously in this chapter), you can then spread them across a "choice of yeses" to engage the buyer in the best outcome for the client.

> Never place a buyer in a "go/no go" dynamic, and never be constrained by a stated budget. If you really believe it's about value, then any budget can be adjusted by a buyer who perceives greater value than expected.

Here's a terrific hint for getting a fee even above the buyer's stated budget. When you provide the options, cite two that are within the budget and one—with even greater and perhaps irresistible value—above the budget. If a client can "find" $175,000 for a project, that client can "find" another $50,000, if warranted. You never know until you ask. No client will ever say, "Be sure to quote me something above my budget." But with the "choice of yeses" approach, you can justifiably do that by providing options within the budget and an additional one that happens to be over the budget but also provides far greater value.

If you don't believe that this approach will work, consider how many times you've bought "extras" for your car, computer, phone, garden equipment, pool, or other possessions that you scarcely wanted at the time, but then realized you couldn't live without. If the manufacturer or catalog or store clerk hadn't brought them to your attention, you still wouldn't own them.

Here are ten guidelines for options, or the "choice of yeses":

1. It's okay to discuss possible options during conceptual agreement, but never, ever assign any fees to them. Simply impress on the buyer that he or she will have choices to make with varying degrees of value and/or protection against risk.
2. Don't "bundle." You're better off "unbundling." Most consultants don't have options because they place every single thing they are able to deliver in their "go/no go" proposal, as if that's the only way to justify their value.
3. Keep a good distance between options. You don't want a mere $5,000 of separation. Each one must represent significantly more income to you.
4. Commensurately with option number 3 above, make sure that each option *clearly provides additional, unquestioned value to the buyer.* Simply promising more of something, or greater frequency, is not value added, but time and materials added. For instance, in my example above, there is no option for additional focus groups or interviews. Each option is clearly distinct.

5. Some options may include prior, lower value ones, and others may stand alone no matter which prior option is chosen. In my example, options 1, 2, and 3 are mutually exclusive, each higher one containing the former; but options 4 and 5 can be applied to any of the first three.

6. Cite your options formally in your proposal, under a category such as "methodology and options."[6]

7. Don't attach fees to the options. Cite the fees separately in the proposal under a category such as "terms and conditions." This is because you want the buyer to focus solely on the value of each option, and not immediately connect it with investment. Let the buyer make a mental choice prior to introducing the fee.

8. If a buyer says, "I like option three, but I only have budget for option two," reply, "Fine, then option two it is." This is not a negotiation.

9. If a buyer asks for a slightly lower fee within an option, reply, "Fine, but what value would you like me to remove?" NEVER decrease a fee without decreasing perceived value.

10. Keep your options relatively simple. This is not rocket science. And be prepared to show the differences in value (and/or the decrease in project risk) as you escalate up the choices.

Don't use a fixed-fee formula. But do have some guidelines that you can apply until you're comfortable moving away from the "science" and toward the "art."

SOME FORMULAS FOR THE FAINT OF HEART

I'm always being asked, "Well, you must really estimate days, right?" Wrong. I only estimate client value and my contribution to it.

I'm aware, however, that many of you will prefer help in the form of analytic science until the more intuitive art kicks in. (Don't forget that there is

---

[6]For a formal template and illustrations, see my book, *How to Write a Proposal That's Accepted Every Time* (Kennedy Information, 2000).

nothing wrong or unethical about the art form of value-based fees *so long as the client believes that the resultant value more than justifies the investment in your help in gaining it.*)

So, for the first time anywhere, here are a formula and some other criteria for establishing value-based fees. While the engineers in the audience won't be pleased ("What's after the fourth decimal place?") and the lawyers will be discomfited ("What, exactly, do you mean by a 'fee'?"), I think the rest of you will at least be happy with the framework.

The Step-by-Step Choice of Yeses

Step #1. Establish the value with the economic buyer in the conceptual agreement phase, after ascertaining objectives to be achieved and the measures of progress. (Questions to ask for the conceptual agreement components appear in the appendices.)

Step #2. Establish your own value based on your uniqueness (why you, why now, why in this manner).

Step #3. Create your options, clearly delineated by increasing value. They may be cumulative or mutually exclusive.

Step #4. Given the value of the project, estimate a profound and significant return on the investment, working backward. In other words, if the buyer has stipulated to a $2 million dollar savings annualized, then a return of 20 to 1 *on the first year alone* would be represented by a $100,000 investment.

Step #5. Create your "choice of yeses" using that conservative, 20 to 1 return rate *as your least expensive option.* Increase your other options by a factor of a minimum of 20 percent. In this case, option 2 would be $120,000, and option 3 would be $144,000 (20 percent above option 2), etc.

Step #6. Now, go back to Step #2. If your own unique value is high on the why me/why now/why in this manner scale, add another 20 percent to each option. If your uniqueness is moderate, add 10 percent. If your uniqueness is low, don't add anything above the Step #4 calculations.

Step #7. Look at the project objectives and value to the organization in their entirety, and then review your fees resulting from the above steps. Ask yourself, "Is this a good deal—a bargain—for the client *in view of the value,* and is it a good deal for me in terms of large margins? If not, adjust up or down, but by no more than 15 percent. If so, then submit it.

Step #8. Stop worrying. You'll close about 60 to 80 percent of these, which is better than your prior rate (don't lie) and at higher profitability.

The "formula" is simple, but the toughest part of this sale is to yourself, not to the buyer.

If you must use a formula, fix it at 20 to 1 or better—in other words, 10 to 1 is just fine. Bolster your case with these beliefs (mainly for yourself):

- The client is probably spending more on warranties for copy machines and ruined postage than for your project.
- The value to the organization, if anything, is probably understated and conservative.
- Your fees are highly conservative (actually, a 5 to 1 return would be a great investment).
- You've probably underestimated your own uniqueness for this client.
- The value is based on first-year returns. The annualized basis would probably represent a return of 100 to 1.
- It doesn't matter whether you could have done it for $20,000 less or the client would have paid $20,000 more. The margins are still terrific for you and the benefits still terrific for the buyer. That is all that matters.

If it appears that the toughest "sell" is to yourself, you've read between the lines quite accurately.

The key to even this formulaic approach is to work *backward* from the ultimate client value, through your unique contribution, to the current fee schedule spread over options. Do not work *forward,* trying to calculate the amount of time, the number of days, the volume of deliverables, or the variety of tasks. They are commodities and, no matter what margin you add to these activities and commodities, it will be miniscule compared to your margin for a truly value-based approach.

The most conservative and even timid value-based approach will be far more lucrative to you, while highly attractive to the buyer, than the most aggressive time and materials calculation. Stop selling yourself short.

The formula presented here is meant as a "halfway house," enough science to get you through until the art form becomes second nature.

CHAPTER 4 ROI

- Conceptual agreement is at the heart of the value-based billing process. Any time invested in gaining conceptual agreement, based on a trusting relationship with a true economic buyer, will actually speed the sale at higher margins.
- Your own uniqueness is an essential component that only you can calculate. But it's as much based on self-esteem and self-belief as it is on any pragmatic background or history.
- The reciprocity of the "good deal" creates the win/win dynamic. The client deserves a good deal, but so do you. One is incomplete without the other.
- The "choice of yeses"—options—is the key tactic in moving a buyer to a consideration of value-based fees, and the propensity will be to move upward through increasing value. Never submit a proposal without options of distinctly different value propositions.

Use the fee formula until you get comfortable, then let the art overtake the science. Remember that you never have to justify your fee basis to a client, and only low-level people will usually make such a demand. You only have to demonstrate the value of the outcomes. Fee setting is a time to be aggressive, not defensive.

If you can't articulate your own value, you can't very well suggest value-based fees. Look in the mirror and practice on the toughest buyer of all. The first sale is to yourself.

How to Convert Existing Clients

Correcting Your Own Mistakes

T he second most popular question I receive after "How do I create value-based fees?" is "How do I move existing clients from hourly billing to value-based fees?"

The answer is: "Very carefully."

You've spent a considerable amount of time educating those clients incorrectly—and you've been very effective at it. You've also consistently enabled their behavior by replying to their demands for hourly or daily rates, reductions in rates, reductions in time, and perhaps reduction in numbers of people. They've become quite comfortable utilizing your services in the manner maximally beneficial to them and minimally beneficial to you.

Furthermore, you're highly credible! After all, your advice has been well-received, your suggestions well-taken, and your plans well-thought-through. Why shouldn't your billing scheme be as adept and effective as your consulting expertise?

Fortunately, that's the extent of the bad news. (I know, that's sufficient!) You've also developed a solid relationship with a buyer who would probably be very loath to see you leave, no matter how much he or she has protested against your fees and rates in the past. You also have a client base that permits you to set some criteria for which clients may be most suitable for "transfer" to a new billing arrangement. Finally, you're successful enough so that you might want to "fire" some clients rather than keep working with them on a basis that is unfair to you.

Nothing raises fees like your willingness to walk away from business. But remember, the first sale is always to yourself. While you don't want to take bread off the table, you also don't want your time so entangled with low-profit clients that you can't work for more and tastier bread in the future. We'll deal with that contingency in this chapter as well.

SETTING PRIORITIES AMONG EXISTING CLIENTS

The first order of business is to establish the decision criteria to determine which clients to even approach. A general "triage" system works best:

1. High potential clients for change to value-based projects
2. Clients who could go either way, but require more work
3. Clients who will not change short of nuclear war

To establish who's who on your list[1] I've established the template below. If the answer is "strongly believe it," give that item a "3"; if the answer is "possibly," give that item a "2"; and if the answer is "strongly doubt it," give that item a "1."

---

[1]Since this series is aimed at highly successful consultants, my assumption is that your firm has a dozen to two dozen active clients and another dozen to two dozen periodic clients. But even if you have fewer than that, the criteria will still apply and you should use them to differentiate among your buyers.

> It's almost impossible to convert all current clients to value-based billing, but it's always possible to convert a few if you carefully establish your targets.

So take any of your existing clients and apply them to the following template:

Test to Determine Potential to Shift a Client to Value-Based Fees

Answer yes or no. Does the client or has the client:

A. Represent significant long-term business potential? _____

B. Generally accepted your prior fee schedule with little protest? _____

C. Provided you with a very senior or high level buyer? _____

D. Have multiple buyers you have sold to or can sell to? _____

E. Represent an organization you would hate to lose? _____

F. Shown a tremendous return on your consulting work? _____

G. Paid you promptly and never debated charges or fees? _____

H. Ever indicated, "Just do it and send us the bill"? _____

I. Have a buyer with whom you are especially close? _____

J. Serve as a reference or exemplar for other clients? _____

Total Yeses: _____

Here is the scoring key:

- *23 to 30:* high potential and deserves a change strategy
- *14 to 22:* moderate potential; approach after first priorities
- *0 to 21:* don't even waste the time

Depending on your client base, you might have as few as three or four candidates, or as many as a dozen or so. The key is to approach each one with a clear and customized strategy (which we'll talk about in the following sections). But the good news is that you've been able to establish some parameters for your efforts. In essence, the top priorities can't be lost, so while the goal is to move them to a value-based system, the "must" is not to drive them away.

Conversely, the bottom tier companies aren't worth your time anyway. (One of my tenets is to deliberately abandon the bottom 15 percent of your business at least every two years, and these are your candidates. See my book *Million Dollar Consulting* for the details.) You could, theoretically, simply announce a change in your billing to them and allow the majority to disappear. (They may well be one-time clients in any case.) Those in the middle will require individual decisions, but their potential isn't high enough to demand that kind of attention at the moment. You might as well continue to collect hourly rates until you're ready to deal with them.

Once you've identified the top priorities with which to attempt conversion, you can build those plans into your normal visits. In other words, you can lay the groundwork during your regular interactions with the buyer, rather than spring the "new approach" on the buyer in one fell swoop.

> Your best business is that which you don't want to lose at any cost, yet also that which you most want to convert to a true value-based approach. Just because of the former fact, don't abandon the latter need.

That groundwork can be laid with the following dialogue, observations, and reminders with the buyer:

- "Your people indicate they'd like to call on me more often, but they're justifiably sensitive to 'running up a bill' every time they need me, despite the fact that I can provide immediate help."
- "Neither one of us can estimate how much time your request is going to require. I think we need to 'stop the meter' so that we can both invest whatever is necessary."

- "I've begun a new relationship with new clients, and I'd be remiss if I didn't offer it to my best clients. Could we put some time aside to discuss it on my next visit?"
- "I know you've been somewhat unhappy about a 'meter running' and uncapped costs. I'd like to suggest a way to change that dynamic that will help both of us."

Before we turn to the actual strategies, please keep these three critical factors in mind:

1. *Every* piece of new and potential business should be treated exclusively and only as a value-based prospect. Never offer any other kind of arrangement to new clients. Educate them correctly from the beginning.
2. The first sale is always to yourself. You must convince yourself first of the advantages to the buyer before you can effectively employ this change strategy.
3. While the idea is to retain the client at all costs, you can't be fearful. Enthusiasm, assurance, and absolute belief carry the day. Hesitancy, tentativeness, and uncertainty will waste everyone's time.

OFFERING NEW VALUE

The most important and effective method for converting existing clients to a value-based fee system is to offer new value. There is no reason in the world for a client to move from your hourly or daily rate to a fixed fee for the exact same value the buyer is now receiving. Think about it: If people change only in accordance with their own self-interests, then "What's in it for them?" Why abandon a clear, reasonable (that is, cheap), and long-standing billing arrangement?

Well, you abandon it if a new system provides more value and better appeals to your self-interest. I'm going to say that again: *You abandon an old system if a new system provides more value and better appeals to your self-interest.*

If you focus on nothing else, focus on that. What "new value" can you offer the buyer in the next phase of the project, in a new project, or in the negotiation of a new agreement that will at least cause him or her to consider moving to a value-based system? Remember our graphic from the first chapter, repeated in Figure 5.1.

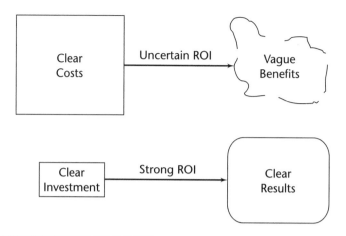

Figure 5.1. Revisiting ROI

We have to create a dynamic in which the buyer appreciates the greater value inherent in a new, clear set of benefits so that the investment is extraordinarily reasonable.

You can't change your billing basis without creating a different *value basis* for the buyer. So focus on the latter in order to create the former.

Here are some generic methods to provide increased value within existing clients (whether new projects—which are easier—or existing projects up for expansion or renewal). You can further modify and strengthen these with specific details for each unique client relationship.

Unlimited Access

Provide "unlimited access" to you. That's not as severe as it sounds. At the moment, the client must make an investment decision every time you're needed ("Is this problem and Alan's help worth $2,500?"). That's a terrible position for the buyer to be in. Offer access at any time, subject to mutually convenient schedules, by phone, fax, email, or in person, if needed.

No client will abuse this privilege (just as no executive was ever prohibited from performing by too many people walking through an "open door"). However, it does provide the immediate perception of far more extensive interaction for a fixed fee.

New Services

Let's say that you've been doing executive coaching. Introduce a 360° feedback intervention, and tell the buyer that you'd like to combine, in the buyer's best interests, the existing coaching work and the new instrument into a single fee for management coaching services. If you're helping with strategy formulation, offer a planning process that bridges to implementation. If you're doing diversity audits, offer a training package for managers to use the feedback properly.

New services, which might seem prohibitive on a per diem, cumulative basis, will seem like a bargain when combined with ongoing services under a single fee for a finite time frame.

Wider Access

Demonstrate that the results you've been generating for the financial area can be readily duplicated in other support areas: human resources, MIS, legal, and so forth. But show that the current hourly basis will be unnecessarily severe, since a great deal of the work is repetitive.

Offer to combine as many other operations as requested under a single fee (even if various budgets contribute to it).

Combined Buyers

If your projects typically involve several buyers who each contribute to the budget, then suggest that, by operating under a single fee, their respective contributions are capped, they no longer have to battle about who should pay for which aspect, and that you can be responsive to all of them without additional investment.

Value-based fees can be strong compromises for the client who is unsure which budgets should be used, how to charge back time, and how often to take advantage of the consultant as a resource.

> You are capable of offering much more value than you currently are providing. You're probably in a rut no better than your client in terms of your utilization. Make sure YOU know the total value offerings you can provide before approaching the client.

New Access Points

Perhaps you can provide a special set of web pages to that client only, using a password; or you can create a newsletter oriented toward the client's employees; or you can arrange a special 800 number; or you can place the client's logo in books that are ordered from you. As part of a value-based proposition, find new and unique access points so that the client feels a more comprehensive relationship.

Don't be afraid to ask the buyer what he or she would find most desirable in terms of a more comprehensive, sustained, and interactive partnership. You may be able to provide the desired service at virtually no cost, but use it as the basis for a higher, value-based fee.

Finally, discipline yourself to "unbundle" the potential value propositions that you can deliver to a client. Use an easel sheet, or a spread sheet, or even a colleague to help you determine the full array of services you can deliver. I guarantee you that: (a) it's far more than you think or (b) it's all combined into a single, grand alternative that you deliver each time.

PRACTICUM

List on an easel sheet a minimum of twenty services, products, advice, and other value propositions that you are capable of delivering. It doesn't matter if they're currently "bundled," if you never provided them before, or if your buyer has never asked about them.

Simply list everything you possibly can, and then cull them down to the most powerful dozen (but keep more if you feel strongly about others). These are your core value propositions, and they can be used in any combination to help convert time-based clients to value-based projects.

FINDING NEW BUYERS
WITHIN EXISTING CLIENTS

If you operate in the small business market (under $50 million in revenues), then there probably is a single buyer who is the owner or CEO. But in larger markets, there are scores or even hundreds of buyers. The problem is that we don't reach out laterally while we're effectively delivering our consulting help.

A new buyer within an existing business does not necessarily have to undertake a project with you on the same basis as others have. The important strategy is to refrain from educating the new buyers incorrectly, as you have the existing buyers!

The advantages of new buyers within existing businesses include:

- No marketing or cost of acquisition
- They have heard of you or can readily become familiar with your work elsewhere within that client system
- They respect and know the people who have hired you in the past
- They are probably not familiar with prior billing policy
- It's easy to see them and to accommodate their schedules, since you're onsite frequently
- Results you've generated elsewhere can be made relevant for them

Most consultants refrain from reaching out to new buyers because of self-imposed limitations. As long as you're doing a good job for the current client, why should anyone object?

Remember that buyers are seldom perched solely at the very peak of the organizational hierarchy. They need to fill only two criteria:

1. Does your value proposition enhance their goals (their self-interests) professionally and/or personally?
2. Can they write a check to acquire that value?

I've seen consultants virtually wade through groups of potential buyers while hurriedly on their way to get to the cafeteria. You have to be willing to market while you're on the client site.

How do you do that gracefully? Well, if you believe that new buyers within the client organization represent new sales that can be placed on a value basis, then they deserve quite a bit of effort. Here are six tactics to reach them efficiently and effectively:

1. Ask your current buyer for recommendations. This seems like anathema to many consultants, but a pleased buyer should have no hesitation about sharing your value in the company so long as that buyer is not short-changed. (In fact, in terms of self-interest, the buyer can often claim credit for "discovering" you.) The salient point here is to *ask* and to even seek an introduction. This is the single most overlooked avenue of expanded business and potential conversion business (to a value basis).

2. Seek out meetings at which to present your reports and suggest that "interested others" and support groups attend. I've presented results at any number of management meetings where people have come up to me and asked, "Can you do that same thing for a support organization?" or "Is it possible to do that overseas?" Guess what? It always is.

3. Listen for key names of power brokers and, when you find yourself with them for any reason at all, introduce yourself. After a second or third encounter, ask them for some time to discuss the ramifications of your work in their area.

4. Publish in the organization's house organ or, even better, allow them to interview you and discuss the results of your work. I once received a six-page, color spread in Merck's in-house magazine on my ethics audits, which brought inquiries from managers I had never even heard of. This is a very effective, objective way to reach out to other buyers.

5. Offer to brief support units, internal customers, internal suppliers, and any other even remotely interested parties. Explain to your client that a synopsis of your work might help others to help your client and that sharing the work will certainly earn admiration in any case. One-on-one or small group briefings are usually the best, since you want to focus only on potential decision makers.

6. Volunteer within the company. I've donated to company-sponsored charities, attended award ceremonies, participated in picnics and recreational opportunities, and tried to become a "part of the crowd." You never know who you'll wind up meeting in comfortable, social, and convivial circumstances.

Finding new buyers within existing clients is essential for any highly successful consultant, but absolutely critical for the consultant who wants to convert existing, high potential hourly clients into long-term value-based clients.

> We tend to view change as threatening. We must view it as opportunity. Every client change represents a potential new piece of business. But you can't just sit back to see what happens. We're not here to put our toe in the water. We're here to make waves.

FINDING NEW CIRCUMSTANCES

The final tactic for converting clients to value-based pricing is to find some new client, market, or environmental circumstance that supports the reasoning for such a change at this particular juncture.

Some new circumstances will be obvious, but others are more subtle. Yet all can serve as your "transfer mechanism." Here are some examples:

The Great Year. The client has had an outstanding year, not least in part to your assistance. Suggest to the buyer that this is a time to consider a more comprehensive and flexible relationship. Also, never neglect the fact that, at the end of any budget year, there are funds often crying to be used or lost. It's tough to put those funds against hourly billing that is not based on any specific amount of hours, but it's relatively easy to put those funds against a clear, $100,000 project.

The Horrible Year. Your client might have had a disaster, not due to anything you did, of course. There might have been some client defections, unexpected costs, loss of technology, or whatever. If the client is happy with your help, however, suggest an easier and less burdensome way to work with you next year, since the fees will be capped, fixed, and otherwise locked in cement. That way, you can't be part of an escalating cost problem, and you can't be cut to try to respond to one. That's win/win.

The New Buyer. Most consultants search for arsenic when their buyer is promoted, fired, replaced, transferred, or otherwise misplaced. But this is really an opportunity to educate a new buyer correctly, rather than try to re-educate an old one used to his or her habits. View a new buyer as an opportunity, and don't allow past practices to continue (hourly fees) without strong resistance (in the form of the buyer's self-interest).

The Acquisition. There is generally chaos when even the best acquisition is contemplated and consummated. Suggest that this is the time to simplify everything possible, including your billing arrangements. The acquisition might also present an opportunity in terms of the other conversion factors (for example, new buyer) discussed above.

The Competition. If the competition has pulled a surprise or the competitive marketplace is heating up, suggest that the increasing demands and uncertainties create an unfair situation for the client on any kind of per diem basis. Since ambiguity makes it nearly impossible to calculate hours or time, offer a set fee to create at least some order out of the uncertainty.

The New Initiative. Almost every organization regularly trots out a new initiative, hot product, reinvention of itself, or some other strategic change (often fostered by a new leader in a key position or the latest academic's fad). Jump on that bandwagon, and use the initiative as an excuse to alter the past fee basis.

The Travel Need. Where travel is a necessary aspect of your project—especially international travel—demonstrate that per diem fees often keep running, although you're just traveling from one place to another. (If you don't charge when you spend two days flying and acclimating to Europe or Asia, you're suffering from more than merely jet lag—you're crazy.) A value-based project fee, including all travel time (although, of course, not travel reimbursement[2]), will remove that unnecessary expense.

Don't take the position that you have to "slip in" an attempt to convert an existing client to a value basis. Use an opportunity or event to demonstrate why it's the perfect time to do so.

Within your existing clients who are still on a time and materials basis, be alert for opportunities to promote a change to value-based fees. In fact, you can use this "new circumstances" approach with your moderate priority clients, as well.

PRACTICUM

Take the high priority clients you arrived at earlier in this chapter and apply the new value/new buyers/new circumstances factors to each. Whichever ones offer the most opportunity in these areas become the highest of the high priority. They should be on your list for an immediate conversion strategy.

Here's another simple formula:

$$\text{new buyers} \times \text{new value opportunities} \times$$
$$\text{new circumstances} = \text{conversion factor}$$

Any factor of three or more represents high potential.

---

[2]There is nothing wrong with including all your projected travel costs in your fee, as long as you feel you have a firm idea of what they will be. That's even a purer billing form, since everything is included.

WHAT IF CLIENTS RESIST A CONVERSION?

Don't push so hard that you cause ill will if your clients resist converting. Position your intent as serving their best interests, and point out that other clients—and all new clients—have chosen to take advantage of the new arrangement. But by offering them this as an option, you're not taking bread off the table, since the client still may choose to continue along the current path.

If your top priority clients resist, here is the course of action that might still win the day later on:

1. Don't persist, but do remind. Once a quarter, remind your buyer that the option is still on the table. Every time one of the conversion opportunities discussed above arises, raise the issue again as the basis for a decision about the new project. There is too much potential profit at stake not to remain persistent, and the more money you make from a client resisting a value-based approach, the more money you are actually *losing* long-term.

2. Appeal to the buyer's sense of fair play. If you can demonstrate a multi-million dollar savings or improvement (see Chapter 4 for objectives, metrics, and value), and you can show that your total hourly fees added up to .001 percent of that improvement (which they well might have), you do have a case to point out that future projects should be more of a win/win endeavor. Many buyers will be reluctant to allow a disproportionate situation to persist if they envision needing your help on an even larger scale in the future.

3. For some clients, you may be able to cite their own methods as a justification for how you should be treated. Does the client charge for value (everyone from auto makers to restaurants actually do), or do they charge by the hour and are themselves unhappy about their own meager profitability?

4. Try to arrive at a "halfway house" by influencing the buyer to commit to a minimum amount of time, guaranteeing you some basic revenue figure. Point out that you've had to put blocks of time aside in anticipation of the client's needs and often short-term demands and that some quid pro quo is appropriate. It's less of a jump from guaranteed fees based on minimum days to value-based projects.

5. Provide the client with some independent endorsement of the value of project fees over time and materials. Use some third-party articles, trade

journals, newsletters, and whatever else you can find that objectively demonstrate to the client that he or she is falling out of step with the times.

If you have a strong relationship with these clients and you continue to deliver results, they have the option of continuing as they have been and there is only a miniscule chance of losing them by asking the buyer to consider a different fee basis. However, you are at great potential risk if you choose not to do this out of fear of losing them, since the more work you obtain, the more profit you are leaving on the table.

You only have 100 percent of your energy and resources to apply. Wasting any amount of this on non-promising and underperforming business is criminally negligent behavior. Thus, you must abandon a portion of your business periodically, because no one else will do it for you. The poorest clients tend to be the most loyal.

ABANDONING BUSINESS

This has remained one of the most controversial concepts I've ever introduced, but also one of the most powerful in providing consultants with the means to acquire higher profit, value-based clients.

We become accustomed to certain kinds of business. We tend not to question that business, but rather to allow it to accrete, as though it is a stalactite growing from the ceiling of our office. It's always been there. Why fret about it now?

Unless we abandon business regularly, we provide ourselves no leeway to reach out for new—and more profitable—business. Our time is usurped and our energies depleted by business that not only can't be converted to more lucrative arrangements, but is actively impeding us from converting (or acquiring) other, more high potential business.

We tend to hang on to certain business with a death grip because:

- It was there when we needed it. Early business that helped pay the bills is not something we easily forget.
- It's easy to do. We don't feel we're really exerting ourselves, so why not? It beats working.
- It's fun. We love the adulation, or the experience, or the environment. Our ego is rewarded and it brightens our day.
- We have an enduring friendship. The buyer and/or others have become friends to whom we feel we owe an allegiance beyond mere business considerations. We don't want to jeopardize that relationship.
- We're throwing good money after bad. We've been promised (time and time again) "exposure" for our earlier, inexpensive work, and we still haven't cashed in. Like poker players who have gone too far in a hand they can't possibly win, we're reluctant to cut our losses.
- We have the time. "Something is better than nothing" (which is NOT true) drives us to accept and perpetuate questionable business.
- We're afraid. "What if other business disappears? How can I have justified cutting this business loose?" Actually, not cutting it loose will cause other business not to appear.
- We're trapped. Scope creep and constant concessions have built up a raft of commitments that we honestly won't ever be able to discharge, not unlike miners who, despite their pay, were forever in debt "to the company store." (Remember the song "Sixteen Tons"? Okay, I'm older than you.)

You simply have to let go in order to reach out. There is no way to both hold on to past, unprofitable business and to acquire future, highly profitable business. Given that mutually exclusive state, is this really that tough a decision?

Abandoning business doesn't have to be as draconian as it sounds. First, make an objective assessment of all of your business every eighteen months or so. (Do it between fiscal years so you won't be influenced by your own planning needs.) Ask yourself these questions about each single client:

- Am I learning regularly?
- Am I still adding value that others can't?
- Am I being paid as well and is my profit as great as with new clients?
- Am I being stretched and forced to grow?
- Am I introducing new products and services on a regular basis?
- Am I using the client as a referral or springboard into other systems?
- Am I enjoying this project and having fun?

If the answer to two or more questions is "no," then plan to move on. It doesn't matter which two.

Next, contact the client and arrange for a constructive transfer to another consultant. There is no need to leave the client high and dry. Simply point out the answers to your own questions ("I'm not learning and I'm no longer contributing unique value") and arrange for someone to take on the project who will see it—at this point in his or her career—as thrilling, subject to further improvement, and lucrative. Remain on board for a time or until the next renewal, or depart as soon as new introductions are made. But get out.

My advice, by the way, is *not* to subcontract this or otherwise take a "piece of the action," such as a referral fee. Doing so ethically obligates you to be accountable for the outcome and may make you, de facto, continually accessible to the client (even if through the new consultant). Cut the cord, forsake the revenue, and move on.

If the client balks about "abandonment," simply point out that it's really in the client's best interest. You can't afford the requisite time any longer, and the client will be better served with "new blood." You're still around in case of emergency, and you can continue whatever social relationships might be in place if you care to.

Danger: If the client responds with an offer of more money, which sometimes happens (because you've been working so cheaply), turn it down cold. The new amount will still be less than your new margin goals, and your time will be usurped as much as, if not more than, before in return for an insignificant increase in fees. Don't be lured by the client's guilty conscience.

Finally, remain in touch and use the client as a reference and referral source. Maintain a friendly relationship, although not a business one. You're actually doing the client a favor, and you shouldn't feel the need to skulk out the door.

Unless you deliberately, proactively, and methodically abandon business, you'll be unable to convert any higher priority clients to a value-based approach, nor will you have the time to acquire new business at the rate or pace that makes sense.

You have to let go to reach out. Let go of those who can most easily go their own way before more important clients let go of you.

CHAPTER 5 ROI

- Existing clients can be converted to value-based clients, but you must set a careful priority.
- Also, never take bread off the table: offer the option to continue the current relationship or to change. Sweeten the latter by pointing out that new clients prefer it, and you'd be remiss if you didn't offer it to existing, important clients.
- Always offer more value, find new buyers, and/or look for new circumstances. The change always must be clearly perceived as in the buyer's best interests.
- You can use a template to determine the highest potential opportunity and then devise a strategy around each particular client.
- Only approach a few at a time, because the process demands careful and rapt attention. The buyer must clearly see the increased value, so be prepared to demonstrate that improved condition (for example, "unlimited access" to your time and expertise).
- The lowest priority clients for conversion are also those who are the highest priority for dropping. Every eighteen months or so, you should systematically examine your client base—again using objective templates and criteria—to determine who you can "let go of" in order to reach out to new and more prosperous business.
- All new business, however, should be considered as value-based prospects and should never be given the option of a time-based or time-and-materials arrangement. By also culling out and setting priorities among your existing business, you should be able to convert your practice to an entirely value-based one in a few short years. That alone will

represent a dramatic increase in your profits without any substantial increase in your work.

Don't try to convert every client to value-based fees, and don't stop trying if some balk or resist. If you convert one or two high-potential clients, you will have created huge, new margins for yourself. Life is about success, not perfection.

CHAPTER 6

The Fine and High Art of Using Retainers

It's Just the Smarts, Stupid

There is a difference in my book (and this is, of course, my book) between value-based fees and retainer fees. While both are in the same ball park, the view of the field is different in this regard:

- *Value-based fees* comprise compensation paid by the client representing the consultant's contribution to the ultimate value (improved condition) that the client agrees will be derived. Value-based fees concern projects of finite scope.
- *Retainer fees* comprise compensation paid by the client representing access to the consultant and the consultant's talents for a specified interval. Retainer fees concern time periods of finite duration.

(Just to keep the record straight, *contingency fees*, which I don't favor for reasons cited earlier in the book, comprise compensation paid by the client as a fixed percentage of a stipulated financial outcome at a certain point in time. Contingency fees concern percentages of monetary gain.)

I've been engaged in retainer fee relationships frequently. I think they make sense under the right conditions, and they can be a wonderful source of ongoing and predictable income in an uncertain and vacillating cash flow profession. However, they can also be dysfunctional and unprofitable if they are not controlled and managed properly.

One final caveat: I *am not* using "retainer" in the lawyer's traditional sense, which is a fixed amount of money from which payment is drawn periodically based on the lawyer's hourly billing rate. That is simply a deposit against hourly bills. "We've retained counsel" actually means "We've paid a law firm a deposit so that they'll show up because they don't trust us to pay them after they show up." If that is what you are intent on doing, go back to Chapter 1.

OPTIMAL CONDITIONS FOR RETAINER ARRANGEMENTS

First, understand that there is no "project" here (there is no "there" there). The client seeks access to your smarts, pure and simple. (Thus, it's not unusual for clients who have engaged you for several successful projects to request you on a retainer basis for the future, but it's unusual—although not impossible—to begin a brand new client relationship on retainer.)

Contrary to the prior sections of this book, the results are not the key consideration here, although they are important. It's the access to your counsel that is the paramount issue. Do not mistake that fact. Your very relationship and the interactions created from it become the value, since there are no specific project results in a true retainer relationship.

You must get comfortable with the idea that access to you is of inherent value. If you don't, the retainer will be an albatross, flying after you everywhere, insisting that you show up, engage in work, clean the tables in the cafeteria, and *demonstrate that you're doing something.*

Notice that I haven't said that a retainer represents your time. Nor have I positioned a retainer as the value of your presence. It's the client's opportunity to approach you—to approach you, not for you to approach the client—that represents the great value here. In other words, don't worry about the nature of the issue, don't worry about the timing, and don't worry about any arbitrary project scope. "If you, buyer, have need for my expertise, just call."[1]

Here are my criteria for the best conditions—those optimally favorable to the consultant—for the establishment of retainer business.

Ten Criteria for Lucrative Retainer Agreement Conditions

1. The Client Is Educated that Access Is the Value.   The client has no intent to use you as a de facto marketing vice president or chief of staff. Nor does the client believe he or she is entitled to see you three days a week, regardless of need. Nor is this a "make work" exercise if you're not actively engaged for a time. The client is paying for your availability and your smarts on an "as needed" basis, no more and no less.

2. The Client Understands that Access Is Not Instantaneous.   You cannot be instantly available. (Try getting your doctor or attorney to be there the moment you need them.) The idea is to create reasonable expectations of access. In my case, I return all calls within ninety minutes, all email within a day, and all correspondence within the week. Onsite work is subject to mutually agreeable scheduling, although appointments planned in advance will always have top priority and are unshakeable in my retainer work. The key aspect of "access" is "responsiveness," not omnipresence.

3. There Is Agreement About Who Has Access.   In most cases, retainers are with a single person. However, there may be times when a team has the access (which costs more and we'll get to below). The people with access must be designated in advance. Otherwise, you can find yourself with a dozen members of

---

[1]We are going to discuss a little later how to handle retainers that magically begin to generate projects that would otherwise engender a value-based fee. So if that's on your mind, just be patient and read on.

the management team demanding your help at all hours and the dreaded "scope creep" has become a demon in what had appeared to be a very effective retainer arrangement.

4. Access Must Be Unlimited for the Client. You can't position some times as more important or convenient than others or declare a block of time "off limits." You would then be driving the client toward certain restrictions, which devalues your access. Actually, when an occasional client calls me on a Sunday night with a special request for advice before an important Monday morning meeting, I'm quite pleased. First, I'm providing tremendous "real time" value; and, second, I'm doing it from the comfort of my home, not having to make a trip to the client. What could be better than that?

> If you don't equate "access" with physical presence, you can actually accommodate quite a few retainer clients at once. Why can't consultants telecommute?

5. Payment Must Be in Advance of the Time Frame. The quid pro quo for unlimited access is payment in advance. If your retainer is for a month, get paid on the first of the month (*not* 30 days, net); if it's quarterly, then get paid at the beginning of the quarter. You cannot run the risk of unlimited access for any significant length of time without payment in your pocket. (The longer the time period, the more the discount. For example, if the monthly retainer is $10,000, then a quarterly retainer option for that client might be $27,000, providing a 10 percent discount; a half-year might be $50,000, but paid in advance.)

6. Boundaries Are Established. You and the client agree on access, but nothing beyond that without further compensation. For example, expenses are extra, as would be any subcontracting required. If the client asks that you conduct a survey or run focus groups or serve in court as an expert witness during the course of the retainer, all of those services and that value demand additional fees. While the access is unlimited, what you will provide after being accessed clearly can't be.

7. The Time Frame Is Finite and Not Turned "On and Off." If the client doesn't access you for two weeks, that's life. You're providing access during a given, finite time frame, not a cumulative time frame of access. The client can't extend the current retainer by saying, "We didn't use you last week." You may, at your option, provide the client with the ability to formally request a "freeze" or "time out" if client business (or personal) demands preclude access to you, but I would do this very sparingly, as in "never."

8. There Is a Clear Renewal Procedure. Repeat business always beats new business (no cost of acquisition), and that holds true in retainer relationships as well. Establish a time frame (for example, the end of the second month of a three-month retainer, or third week in a one-month retainer) during which you and the client can mutually decide to continue for another time frame (or even a more extended one) or, unilaterally, either of you can end the arrangement at the conclusion of the current time frame. It's mutual continuance or unilateral discontinuance. The key here is to allow you to bail out if you wish, but also to guarantee the next time frame and advance payment if all is going well for both of you. Do not wait for the end of the retainer period to do this.

9. Create High Priority Potential Areas of Collaboration. You might indicate to the buyer that you've both agreed that sales retention, or commercialization in R&D, or acquisition evaluation will be the primary focus. In this way, you have the ability to follow up and pursue certain issues with the buyer. Although it may seem ideal, receiving a retainer and not being accessed at all will guarantee just one thing: no renewal business. So if access to you isn't being taken advantage of, then you need a basis for "priming the pump." Those can be established at the outset so you have a reasonable premise for contacting the buyer on occasion.

10. Always Stress that This Is Collaborative. A retainer arrangement generally represents a pure counseling role, an advisory relationship, and a partnership. It is far more like coaching than consulting in that regard. It's about ongoing advice, not temporary "wins" and "losses." Keep your eye (and your client's eye) on the larger picture. A retainer does not fail because a new, highly sought employee leaves for the competition; but it does fail if the client either doesn't access your advice or ignores your advice about a strategy for finding and retaining top talent in a competitive market.

Retainers can utilize a variety of time frames. But they shouldn't be too short or too long. Both extremes threaten the value of the relationship.

CHOOSING TIME FRAMES AND CREATING REALISTIC EXPECTATIONS

Retainers are not ideal for very brief or very long durations, unless they are periodically renewed, and even those have problems caused by their very longevity.

First, retainers that are too short don't give the buyer enough time to access your help under a variety of conditions, to allow truly valuable applications for your advice to arise, and/or for you to become adept at this particular arrangement with this particular buyer. I believe that the absolute minimum time frame for a retainer is a month, but two months is far better and a quarter is ideal. For a single month, the buyer could encounter an event that usurps all of his or her time, and you might not be called on at all. (Even though you could choose to extend the retainer "on the house," it sets a bad precedent.)

Second, however, overly long retainers cause the buyer to question the value if you've become so successful at advising (and transferring your skills to the buyer) that toward the end of the arrangement there is much less contact and much less *perceived* value on the buyer's part.

I believe that the fairest retainers are probably for ninety-day periods and they can renew at the end of sixty days on the same terms (if the client demurs, but then wants to renew after the retainer is completed, you're perfectly justified in raising the retainer fee—that's why the sixty-day option is there as part of the client's benefit). If you feel strongly about six months, so be it; there's nothing writ in stone here. But you are probably far better off with two years' worth of retainer that has renewed every quarter or every half-year than you are with attempting two annual ones.

The problems, however, with even long-term, frequently renewed retainers include:

- You become perceived as the buyer's "hit man" (hit person?) and not as an objective observer.

- You really have come to represent a single interest and a single point of view. You've probably developed a social, or at least personal, relationship with the buyer.

Long-term retainers can turn you into a member of management, which immediately devalues your role as a consultant and, therefore, ultimately undermines your fee structure.

- One of your initial high value components, objectivity, is lost when you become so familiar and so immersed in one client that your nose is pressed too tightly against the glass.
- The retainer account may actually become eligible for that bottom 15 percent that requires jettisoning (see the prior chapter) because it's no longer interesting, you're no longer learning, and you no longer bring energy and innovation to the equation.

VIGNETTE

I had been working on retainer for Calgon in the 1990s for four years at $100,000 per year. In October of the fourth year, as was our custom, the CEO and I met to discuss the following year. "Let's do it again," he said simply.

"Okay, I'll send you the paperwork with the same terms," which meant that I would invoice him for $100,000 in December, which he could put into either the current or the next fiscal year.

"No, not the same terms," he said, and I was jolted a bit, since I had thought the relationship was as good as it had ever been, and we had tackled some tough issues over the past year. "Raise it by a third; you're undercharging me," he said, after a short pause.

It was one of the few times in my life that I was speechless. But I still managed to send the larger invoice without a problem.

(Of course, it's a rare client who will suggest this, so I wouldn't depend on my degree of passivity!)

In a more conventional, value-based project, you set expectations by establishing objectives, measures, and value to the client (conceptual agreement in my lexicon—see Chapter 4). In a retainer relationship, you still must carefully establish expectations, but in a different manner. Remember, the access, not the particular project, constitutes the value.

Quick Tips for Gaining High-Value, High-Profit Retainers

Here are some guidelines to use to set the optimal conditions for success with a buyer in a retainer relationship:

1. Define "access." It doesn't mean "always on" or instant availability.
2. Provide unique value to the access. You might provide your home, cell, and car phone numbers, which are normally never provided (nor should they be) to conventional clients.
3. Set your calendar to intervene in silences. If you haven't heard from a buyer in, say, ten days, I'd make a call or send an email, just to remind the buyer that you're there if needed. Just that gesture can help substantiate your value, even if the client hasn't called you.
4. Ask the client for unique access. Is there a way to circumvent a secretary or voice mail? Might you have the buyer's home number? Is there an unscreened email address?
5. Go above and beyond in an obvious manner. Let the client know you'll move something non-critical to meet the buyer's urgent schedule. Review a lengthy report overnight, even though it's an imposition. Talk to a client's customer whom the client is afraid of losing, even if it's not an agreed on part of the deal.
6. Don't promise too much. You can't really reduce turnover, improve sales, or increase market share on this basis. (You can take on projects in those areas, but see the next section in this chapter for advice on the best ways to accommodate—and charge—for that.) What you can do is give the buyer peace of mind and improved skills, as well as validation for the buyer's thinking.
7. Remember that, as a consultant, you seldom surprise people who know what they're doing. In other words, merely verifying that a position or

course of action makes sense to you as an objective outsider is often sufficient. You don't have to help the client invent a new Post-it® Note.

8. Do some studying. Although I've stated often that consultants are process experts and not, necessarily, industry or content experts, it nonetheless helps when you become more proficient in the type of business that has hired you on retainer. Read the trade magazines and do an Internet search periodically. Learn your client's lingo, and study your customer's customers.

9. Push back as needed. You're not there to salve the buyer's ego, but to help make the buyer successful. Take risks. Jeopardize the relationship if it means saving the buyer from himself.

10. Finally, be willing to walk away. It's unethical to sit back and keep the money if you believe that a long-term retainer isn't working. Sometimes, you and the buyer made a mistake. Think of future business and future referrals, and suggest that the current arrangement be ended with a pro-rated refund or credit toward future projects. This is the height of professionalism, and it justifies high fees.

Not all retainers will work out well, even when undertaken with great respect and mutual investment. If it's not working, then it's much better for you to suggest that it end. Always think of future business, not your current bank account.

ORGANIZING THE SCOPE AND MANAGING PROJECTS WITHIN THE RETAINER

One of the most common problems with retainer assignments is that more traditional consulting projects "crop up" in their midst, like mushrooms after a thunderstorm. One day you're on retainer, and the next you're surrounded by projects.

Consultants generally worry that their retainer has become a "catchall" for projects that, in and of themselves, would represent more lucrative assignments if taken on in a value-based billing system. And they're right.

You have to make clear to the client that any discrete projects that may arise during the retainer's time frame are *not* included in the fee for the retainer itself, and this is easier said than done. The major problems and challenges follow, and they shouldn't be taken lightly, because they affect your effectiveness for the client and, quite realistically, your income.

The client will tend to view you as a resource—almost as an employee—who can be "assigned" as the client sees fit, if you don't counter that notion early in your retainer "education." That's why I've stressed *access* as your value (figuratively, the ability to "pick your brain") and not *projects.* The client can't think that the retainer is only showing a return on investment if you are actively engaged in some activity. You have to draw a clear line in the sand from the outset. For example, if you choose to take on an early project within the retainer at no additional fee "just to get things underway," you're setting a precedent and creating an expectation that will kill you.

As you hear of and/or advise on projects that should be undertaken (for example, something the buyer has asked your advice on indicates that the human resources function needs to be audited and overhauled), and the buyer understands that any projects you undertake are *in addition to* the retainer, it can be construed that you're actually trying to leverage your retainer into more business. My solution: As you (and you will) identify potential projects and initiatives that the client should consider, *always* suggest ways that the client could do it internally or with some other external resources. Don't recommend yourself. (Some consultants refuse to enter into project work themselves while on retainer, which I find an extreme as ridiculous as including projects within the retainer.) If the client wants you, nonetheless, even after being presented with alternative resources, then you can legitimately take the work on at a project fee.

You can lose money on retainers if you consider yourself a one-person "SWAT team" who is all things to all people. Retainers, like projects, have limits and parameters. If you don't know them and articulate them, you can be sure the client won't think about it at all.

You're best served if you create a policy for any project work at the outset, which will also contain a beneficial financial aspect for the client.[2] For example, stipulate at the outset that a project will have these characteristics:

- Clear objectives, measures, and value (conceptual agreement) to be achieved during a finite interval
- A separate proposal signed off by the buyer and the consultant
- An agreement that the project and retainer work will complement, and not compete with, each other
- A separate payment schedule, which will feature a strong discount for the project work in view of the ongoing retainer project (My advice here is to give increasingly steep discounts for longer retainer periods. In other words, a project during a quarterly retainer might justify a 20 percent discount, but a project during an annual retainer might justify a 33 percent discount.)

You want to create a win/win dynamic for projects undertaken while a retainer is in force, causing the client to appreciate that the project required additional investment but that the investment is lessened by the retainer relationship.

Because a retainer usually symbolizes an excellent relationship with the buyer and strong, mutual trust, it won't be unusual for the client to suggest project work during the retainer period. In fact, the retainer arrangement might be the natural result of several highly successful buyer/consultant collaborations. Consequently, it's all the more important to separate the two efforts, lest the buyer simply (and logically) conclude that it's far less expensive to pay you a single fee to work on multiple projects than it is to pay you for each project! If you don't take pains to correct this impression—or better, to prevent it—a retainer arrangement can actually *ruin* what was a fine relationship engendered by those projects.

---

[2]Obviously, these aren't major concerns for short-term (for example, one month) retainers. But a project can surface at any time, and most surely will during a ninety-day or six-month period.

Retainer *scope* is also an important consideration. In other words, it's proper to define the parameters of the retainer's "reach." Are you on retainer to the sales department, which your buyer heads, or to anything the sales vice president is charged with (for example, a special acquisition project) or has on his or her mind (for example, personal advice and coaching on seeking the senior vice presidential position).

The extent to which you are confined to a single buyer (or single source if a buyer has asked you to work with someone) is critical. If your buyer and presumed single source says, "I want to let Ann borrow you over in R&D because she has some people issues that I know you can help with," you're in trouble. There are probably scores of managers whom you can help with "people issues," and you can't afford to be the "people handyman."

Unless you have a "freeze" option on the retainer, the client has to realize that the retainer *stops* at a certain point, irrespective of the amount of use or lack of use. Educate the client that a few highly valuable interactions are far better than daily, idle chatter. And don't be bashful about mentioning an approaching deadline for the end of the retainer. (This is why I advocate formally discussing the extension or termination of the retainer a month or more prior to its scheduled conclusion date. That way, there are no "blurred" lines as the end approaches.)

By the way, there's nothing wrong with any project work undertaken extending beyond the conclusion of the retainer period. But keep them separate, so that the client doesn't continue to use you as a retainer resource while you continue to work on the project, or as a project resource after the project is over and you continue on retainer.

> The longer the retainer period, the more critical the need for clarity on potential project work, retainer scope, and other areas of ambiguity. It's a good idea to have a simple, one-page document that outlines the parameters of the retainer arrangement.

CAPITALIZING ON RETAINER RELATIONSHIPS

Since referral business is so important in our profession, referrals citing you as an excellent retainer resource can be golden. While it normally may require several successful projects for a client to be comfortable enough to enter into a retainer arrangement, it won't take more than a heartbeat for that client to recommend you to others on that same basis. If you enjoy retainers and the relative freedom and margins they provide, this is a golden opportunity.

As you become accepted on a retainer basis from the outset with new clients, you should continually perfect the relationship so that it makes sense for you and your style. For example, you may want to simply remain on retainer, or you might seek to use retainers to leverage into additional project work. Both are legitimate strategies.

I suggest that, if you do frequent retainer work, you develop a one-page "working agreement" in addition to your proposal that you and the client agree on after the deal is signed but prior to work beginning. This provides the advantage of keeping the simple document out of the potentially trivializing grasp of the legal department, and allows it to be the informal template that you and the buyer use to guide the retainer relationship. An example of such a letter is on the next two pages, but it's meant only as a guide and not as the last word. Customize it to your particular comfort and situation.

A simple working agreement, tailored to your style and preferences, is an ideal discussion point at the outset of the retainer relationship. I often call the points in the agreement the "rules of engagement."

AGGRESSIVELY MARKETING RETAINER RELATIONSHIPS

Once you have the experience of several retainers under your belt, you may want to include the service as a focal point of your marketing "gravity." (Don't forget that if you engage in executive coaching on a value-billing basis, you may well have created a retainer arrangement without realizing it.) This means that you may want to undertake the following marketing efforts:

- Include testimonials in your press kit and on your website that refer to the benefits of your having been on retainer (not only on your overall quality)

Letter of Agreement for the Retainer Relationship
of Alan Weiss on Behalf of Summit Consulting Group,
and Grace Jones, Vice President of Marketing for Acme Corporation

1. The retainer is for the six-month period from July 1 to December 31, 2002.

2. Your access to me is unlimited during the retainer period and under our single fee. My business and personal contact information (phone, fax, email, street address) appear below for your exclusive use. You will provide me with personal and direct contacts to you to expedite our communications.

3. The retainer fee will be paid upon commencement and is non-refundable for any reason. However, you may request a "freeze" of the calendar at any time in intervals of thirty days, which will be added to the end of the retainer period. The ultimate limit of the retainer period will be March 31, 2003, under any circumstances.

4. The retainer fee represents access to my advice, counsel, and coaching for you, personally, in your capacity of vice president of marketing and also for your special assignment to choose a new advertising firm.

5. Any specific projects which you and I agree I might undertake on behalf of the company shall be in addition to this retainer arrangement and will require a separate set of objectives, metrics, and fees expressed in a separate proposal. We agree that a specific project is represented by an initiative that requires more than my advice and counsel to you, as indicated by a clear set of business objectives (for example, improved retention of sales talent) to be

- Place "typical results" achieved from your retainer work, specifically, on the website and in your press kit
- Conversationally mention your retainer work in speeches. For example, "When I was on retainer to the executive vice presidents of several trade associations, I found that their common challenge was increasing membership in a strong economy when everyone was attending to their own businesses . . ."

achieved. I will always suggest alternative methods to engage in such projects with internal resources or other third-party resources at your request.

6. During the month of November, we will discuss the potential of extending the retainer for a similar period at its conclusion. Either of us may decline. If we both decide to proceed, that decision will be made by November 30, 2002, so that I can allocate proper time. The new start date would be January 1, 2003, or at the conclusion of any "freeze" time we have agreed on.

7. You and I will periodically review this working agreement as the retainer progresses and we learn from our work together. We will remain flexible, but we agree that any revisions or changes must be agreed on by both of us.

8. Any expenses incurred during the course of the retainer will be billed at the end of that calendar month as actually accrued and will be due upon receipt of the invoice.

9. The value of our relationship is in our personal, trusting, and unrestricted contact, not in frequency or onsite visits. Let's maximize our efficiency by phone and email, and only meet personally at those times when we can best accomplish our objectives in person. This will reduce your expenses as well as maximize the flexibility of our interactions.

10. Trust is the essential element. I will regard all of our discussions as strictly confidential, covered by non-disclosure agreements, and not to be repeated without your explicit permission. In return, you will keep me apprised of the effectiveness of my help and advice and suggest ways to improve our partnership at any time.

- Write articles on the value of retainer relationships, and/or mention those relationships (as in the speech example above) in your other articles
- Where appropriate, include a retainer option in your proposals—generally most effective when the prospect "doesn't know what he doesn't know" and realizes that help is required to begin sorting out the numerous challenges and opportunities facing the organization

You have the option of occasionally, frequently, or solely engaging in retainer relationships. This is not a client, market, or competitive factor. It's a question of how you choose to structure your practice.

- Consider structuring some of your pro bono work on a retainer basis, even though you're not being paid, that is, become an advisor to the pro bono client, rather than engaging in a particular project or serving in a particular capacity
- Become an "authority" on retainers so that others seek you out; if the profession considers you an expert, clients will, too

How many retainers can you take on at one time? I don't know, and the answer really isn't important or even necessary to know, for the same reason that it's dangerous to have a business plan of 25 percent growth or $5 million in revenues. The danger is that you hit it, when you should have done much better.

I've been engaged in three major retainers at once, in the midst of project work for other clients. I found that not only was it not taxing, but the retainers provided a nice change of pace from my more traditional, project-oriented work. (Not to mention a nice, fixed source of income.) The longest retainer I was ever involved with was for five years with Calgon, and I think that was an aberration created by an exceptional CEO, terrific chemistry, and a surfeit of needs in a very tough, competitive marketplace. (During my tenure there I actually helped with the sale of the company from Merck to English China and Clay.)

My experience and observations would indicate that a consultant could develop a pure retainer practice, with project work the exception, rather than the other way around. It's much more likely and appropriate an event when one's career is in a mature stage, but it's certainly something that can be anticipated and planned for at any stage.

To conclude, here are the traits and abilities that I think are important for the consultant who wants to foster and build more retainer relationships, above and beyond those traits we need in any case merely to be effective consultants.

The Traits of the Successful Retainer Consultant

- *Very Rapid Framing Skills:* The ability to hear your client create patterns, common problems, universal challenges, and so on, which enables you to arrive at relatively few pieces of advice to resolve what may seem like a myriad of issues.
- *Non-Judgmental:* Refraining from commenting on how you would do something or why your client is his or her own worst enemy, but focusing on true evidence and observed behavior, which can be validated and confidently addressed.
- *Empathy But Not Sympathy:* The latter is feeling what the other party feels, but the former is understanding how the other party feels. You need to empathize in order to gain trust, but not sympathize and merely commiserate about misfortune or bad rolls of the dice. You must provide avenues toward success and not rationalizations for failure.
- *Rapid Responsiveness:* While you're not immediately on call and don't need a pager, you should be able to respond to phone requests within a couple of hours and email requests within the same day. Some issues really can't wait and, if you have a particularly hyper or "type A" client, you may be able to save a great deal of grief by heading things off at the pass rather than waiting around the bend.
- *Push Back:* Your client will sometimes be wrong, based on the facts. Tell the client (which is why it's so much better to be paid in advance). Don't equivocate. Tough love is better than soft pity (or cowardice). Confront the behavior and help to change it. A little of this will go a long way.

Not every consultant is an effective retainer consultant. This is not simply an elongated project. It's a more intense and personal relationship, requiring a higher degree of communication skills.

- Retainers are not always the best alternative, but they make a great deal of sense when the client wants access to your smarts. The key is to position the value as having that access.
- Projects may arise that will require a separate proposal and fee. Don't confuse a retainer with the responsibility to accept every project that might come along as being a part of that retainer.
- Establish realistic expectations with the buyer early, and commit them to a letter of agreement post-sale (and post-proposal). That way you can establish "rules of engagement" short of the legal department.
- Quarterly and semi-annual time frames are probably ideal, although monthly and annually can be done well. Anything less than that or more than that is problematic.
- Make sure you create conditions that are maximally supportive of the retainer arrangement. Organize the scope and the parameters so that they are crystal-clear.
- Exploit and capitalize on the retainer success—you may choose to move your practice partially or predominantly in that direction.
- Arrange for retainer renewals well before the period is over. Either party can unilaterally end it, but both are required to extend it.

Your mind and your talent are assets that represent value in themselves. Why not charge for access to such assets? After all, the ultimate brand is you.

Sixty Ways to Raise Fees and/or Increase Profits Immediately

Act Today and Also Receive the Bass-o-Matic Free of Charge

After six chapters on the strategy, rationale, and large-scale tactics for improving your fees, I thought it would be nice to create a brief interlude strictly on street-level tactics that can be employed immediately. (With apologies to all those excellent "guerilla" and "street fighter" books, I don't believe that fee setting is a matter of ambushing clients in alleys or garroting them from the rear.)

You might want to use the techniques that follow as a template, to test your aggressiveness in setting fees. Or you might view them as a buffet, from which you can draw the nourishment that best augments your current diet. Or as an exercise ritual. . . .

That's enough of that. The point is that not one of us, despite our smarts and successes, is doing everything he or she can to maximize our income commensurate with the value we are providing. And while the preponderance of this book deals with the longer term, there is a high probability that you may be leaving money on the table today—right now, as you're reading this—in terms of proposals that are too modest, negotiations that aren't handled assertively, and opportunities that are being lost.

So if you were to review this book twice a year to ensure that your fee strategies are moving ahead in the right direction, you might also review Chapter 7 monthly to ensure that you are not missing something right under your nose. (If you have staff of any kind, it's important that they familiarize themselves with this chapter, because it has implications for everyone from business acquisition people to receptionists.)

Since I've been working on the art and science of fee setting for over fifteen years, and I didn't want to provide anything less than a comprehensive array in this chapter, some of the material has appeared in part and in different forms elsewhere. The two primary sources are the first book in this series, *The Ultimate Consultant*, and my booklet (which started it all) "How to Maximize Fees in Professional Service Firms."

> If you follow my philosophy of The 1 Percent Solution™ then you only need apply one technique to raise fees every day for seventy days to have potentially doubled your income in that period.

And now, on to the techniques. You might want to read a batch at a time and think about them, or highlight or take notes as you go through them. Overlaps and partial duplications are deliberate, since I don't want to miss a nuance that might apply to some and not to others, depending on how I present them and in what context.[1]

---

[1] I have a friend, Greg Godek, who wrote a book called *1001 Ways to Be Romantic*. Someone mentioned to me that he thought there were really only 987, because of fourteen purported duplications. I told him that if he were able to master the 987, he probably wouldn't miss the other fourteen.

THE FIRST FIFTEEN

1. Establish Value Collaboratively with the Client. It's imperative to reach agreement with the buyer as to the real worth to the organization of achieving the business outcomes specified in the objectives. This should be done interactively (that is, not by email or letter), and result with the buyer literally nodding in agreement as you summarize the quantitative (retention improvement) and qualitative (better teamwork) worth, which you can then reiterate in your proposal.

2. If Value Differs, Fees Can Differ. Just because you're doing the exact same thing for two different clients doesn't mean the fee must be the same. Coaching a vice president running a $200 million division and coaching a manager running a $350,000 sales center have two vastly differing outcomes, even if the coaching regimen is the same in each case.

3. Base Fees on Value, Not on Task. Never base a fee on your doing something. Always base it on the client achieving something. Tasks (surveys) are commodities. Value (market share) is a unique client improvement. Also, never base fees on per head (numbers of people in a workshop or survey) basis, which tends to drive the client to limit participation.

4. Forget About What's Happened Before. It doesn't matter if the client has always paid by the day for a certain type of help, or if the client places limits on fees for consultants. No one needed a "fat" pen until Mont Blanc produced them. If you allow yourself to be guided by the client's history, you're helping neither the client nor yourself.

5. Never Use Time as the Basis of Your Value. The toughest obstacle for consultants to overcome is to disregard their time. They tend to believe that the client will abuse their time, or that the time a client demands is time lost elsewhere. In truth, clients don't abuse time if there are clear, delimiting objectives, and the time you would be spending with your feet propped up watching a "Seinfeld" rerun doesn't count. Conversely, you can't feel guilty just because you only had to show up four times to complete a $74,000 project (which has happened to me frequently). You must shake the "time ghost." Your value is in your talent, not in your showing up.

6. Practice Stating High Fees. That's right, practice saying, "It will be between $150,000 and $225,000" out loud. When you say these things matter-of-factly, the client assumes that he or she is out of step if the amount sounds high. When you giggle or turn red, you lose a certain amount of credibility.

7. Think of the Fourth Sale First. Fees are cumulative, not situational. Don't be greedy. Even on a value basis, the goal is to develop a relationship and implement successful projects that will lead to years of work. View your larger clients strategically, and anticipate how you can be of help over years on a variety of projects, not just for the present on a single project. Over 80 percent of my business has been repeat business, and most of the rest has been by referral. The cost of acquiring new business from scratch seriously decreases margins.

8. Don't Use Round Numbers, But Don't Be Ridiculous. It's probably best not to position options at $100,000, $125,000, and $150,000, but it's also ridiculous to cite $123,687.90. The client is going to want to see the worksheet that generated that kind of precision. Remember: If the client walks away thinking that the value was a bargain, and you walk away feeling that you were paid well, there is no third consideration.

9. Engage the Client in the Diagnosis; Don't Be Prescriptive. The client perceives much greater value when you and the buyer are jointly diagnosing the issues, instead of you prescribing some off-the-shelf medicine. Internists make much more money than pharmacists because they are so much more valuable in diagnosing illness. And when the patient is involved in the diagnosis and resultant course of treatment, the quality and success of the treatment are greatly enhanced. One simple way to do this quickly: Provide a "process visual" and let the buyer decide where the organization belongs. See Figure 7.1 for an example.[2] Ask the buyer to profile the organization for each factor.

---

[2]See my book, *The Great Big Book of Process Visuals, or Give Me a Double Axis Chart and I Can Rule the World,* for examples of fifty such process visuals and potential joint diagnostic tools (Summit Consulting Group, 2000).

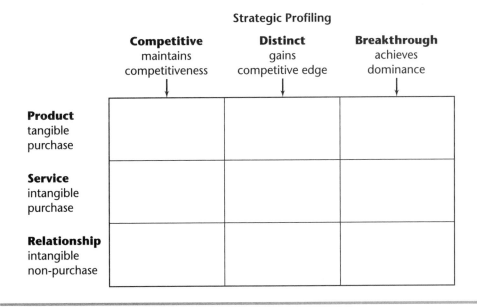

Strategic Profiling

	Competitive maintains competitiveness	**Distinct** gains competitive edge	**Breakthrough** achieves dominance
Product tangible purchase			
Service intangible purchase			
Relationship intangible non-purchase			

Figure 7.1.   Strategic Profiling in Which the Buyer Joins in the Diagnosis

> There is an intrinsic value in merely involving the client in terms of how to approach the project. Value is not based solely on what you do, but also on your embrace of others.

10. Never Voluntarily Offer Options to Reduce Fees.   In a frenzied attempt to close business rapidly, many consultants build in automatic fee reductions, based on numbers, multiple assignments, and other factors. The only option I ever recommend is a small discount for the client to pay the entire fee at the time of project acceptance, and that's mainly for two reasons: You have use of your money from the outset, and the client cannot cancel the project.

11. Never, Ever Deal with a Purchasing Manager or Accounts Payable.   If the buyer suggests that "Finance will take it from here," insist that you and the buyer absolutely agree on the fees and the payment terms. Emphasize that "finance" is fine if they are merely the implementers of the paperwork and generate the checks, but that in your experience someone often tries to show worth by pressuring for a "better deal." While you have the buyer, create agreement on your agreement.

12. Add a Premium if You Personally "Do It All." Often a contract will have a provision that says the consultant will do everything required, but if subcontractors are used the fee will increase to accommodate the extra expense. Presumably, the extra help will speed the project completion. I do just the opposite. I tell the client that the fee is for the entire project and I'll decide on the subcontract help as needed. However, if the client wants me to do all of the work in order to keep a single "filter" in place or guarantee a single qualitative source, then there is a 10 percent premium on the fee. In other words, it costs more if I'm the only one to work on the project, not less. I'm the talent, not the subcontractors.

13. Remove Fees from All Printed Materials. Purge any reference to fees in your printed, web, and other promotional materials. Make sure that old testimonials do not inadvertently provide a fee schedule (for example, "Joan was expensive at $5,000 per day, but a bargain in the long run!").

14. If Forced to Consider Fee Reduction, Reduce Value First. Sometimes reduction of fees is a reasonable request. On those occasions, never reduce fees without making a commensurate decrease in value. Take out the international part of the study, or remove the post-survey discussions with management, or eliminate the written reports. Sometimes a client will say, "We can't afford to lose that" and will concede the fee, but in any case you don't want to be seen as someone who has a padded fee awaiting reduction.

15. Always Make It Clear that Expenses Are "Extra." Except in those cases where you are deliberately including expenses in the fee, state orally and/or in writing that the quote is "plus expenses." Many clients will claim that they thought the fee included *everything*, whether they did or they didn't, and you might be salivating sufficiently on the edge of a "yes" that you agree. Don't. It could cost you thousands on the bottom line.

THE SECOND FIFTEEN

16. *Always Provide an Option that Is over the Budget.* Sometime you'll be told the budget, and it's reasonable, so always provide one option that is above the limit. There will still be two or more options within the budget limitation, so you're not risking anything but just may be creating much higher profits. I lost a piece of business once to a competitor who came in over budget but offered far more than the buyer had specified. I didn't have to learn that lesson twice.

VIGNETTE

"I'm told you're very expensive by my colleague who referred you," said the buyer I had just met at a New York bank.

"I'm not that expensive," I replied, "if you consider the return on investment that this project will provide. It's no different from the returns you seek for your investors."

"Well, we boast about being the best, so I guess that means we'd better acquire the best help around, right?"

There's nothing like a referral system that already educates a prospect about what to expect, nor a prospect who is already positioned to appeal to his own clientele as a high value choice.

17. *As Early as Possible, Ask the QGTRIHF: "What Are Your Objectives?"* This is the "question guaranteed to result in higher fees." Always begin with objectives, because they focus the buyer on results (not on costs) and provide you the opportunity to pursue real needs (not wants). There is nothing easier, nor more valuable, than starting the process by stating, "Can we begin with what you'd like to accomplish as a result of this project?"

18. *Broaden Objectives as Appropriate to Increase Value.* If a buyer says, "We need better market share in the northeast," I always ask, "Wouldn't you want greater market share everywhere?" If the buyer says, "My team needs better delegation skills," I inquire, "What about the skills of their reports in accepting delegation, and the culture of the organization in supporting empowerment?" It's relatively easy to broaden the objectives—and, consequently, raise the fees— by asking a few innocent questions.

19. Ensure that the Client Is Aware of the Full Range of Your Services. Prospects will sometimes jump to a conclusion about your "specialty," or they may have been misinformed by a reference source. If you're talking about a customer survey, for example, don't be reluctant to drop into the conversation that "One survey we conducted was immediately before we ran a strategy retreat, which provided contemporary feedback for the strategy process."

Few things limit fees as much as stereotyping. That's why the concepts of "develop a niche" and "specialize or die" are so constricting. The fewer competencies you, yourself promote, the fewer opportunities for the client to pay you.

20. If Something Is Not on Your Playing Field, Subcontract. My rule of thumb is this: If the predominant aspects of the project are not within your competencies, then refer it elsewhere. But if the predominant parts are within your competencies, then subcontract what you can't handle. It's the overall relationship that counts, not individual mastery of every implementation element.

21. Always Ask Yourself, Why Me? Why Now? Why in This Manner? If the buyer has a raft of choices, you're less valuable, but if you're one of the few with the expertise or repute, you're much more valuable; if the client can wait without problem, that's one thing, but if the window of opportunity is closing, that's quite another; if the client can do this internally, that's easy, but if an external consultant is mandatory, that's different. By asking these questions you'll know your intrinsic value in setting the appropriate fee.

22. Use Proposals as Confirmations, Not as Explorations. Don't submit a proposal until you have conceptual agreement on objectives, measures of success, and value to the organization. Otherwise, the proposal becomes a negotiating document, and the options you have listed will be the point of departure to negotiate downward. I hit over 80 percent of my proposals, but I send out far fewer than most consultants, because of my method of using them.

23. *When Asked Prematurely About Fees, Reply, "I Don't Know."* Don't be cornered. Simply tell the buyer that you can't quote a fee until you have more information—in fact, it would be unfair to the prospect to do so—but you can have the options ready within twenty-four hours. When consultants allow themselves to be forced into fee quotes prematurely, they almost always quote too low a fee, and the prospect expects to negotiate down from there.

24. *If You Must Lower Fees, Seek a Quid Pro Quo from the Buyer.* In the real world, you'll sometimes want a piece of business and will accept a lower fee to get it. Even then, suggest an accommodation where the client guarantees to provide referrals, or videotapes one of your presentations for your use, or provides products and services for free or at cost, or places you in front of a related trade association. There is usually some barter that is attractive to both parties.

> Don't use other people if you don't have to. There is no inherent benefit in numbers or bodies. No matter how much you charge, every additional employee or subcontractor on a project will reduce your margins.

25. *Don't Accept Troublesome, Unpleasant, or Ugly Business.* A prospect who is unethical, ornery, nasty, or otherwise unfriendly won't magically metamorphose as a client. Bad prospects are bad clients, and the only thing worse than no business is bad business. No matter what the fee, these clients will cost you more than you keep.

26. *When Collaborating, Use Objective Apportionment.* You may divide the client business into acquisition, methodology used, and delivery, for example. That means that, if I sell the client, my technology is used, but you deliver; I get two-thirds and you get one-third. Use whatever formula you like (some people

feel the acquisition aspect deserves more weight), but use something that's clear and objective too so that the ground rules are clear for revenue sharing.

27. *Any Highly Paid Employee Must Bring in New Business.* Whether on salary, bonus, and/or commission, high pay is justified for new business acquisition. Delivery, research, and support are commodities for which you should subcontract. In fact, it's a buyer's market, since those abilities are in huge supply. Don't pay people for delivering your business acquisition unless it's on a pay-for-performance basis.

VIGNETTE

A prospect kept gently inquiring about costs during our initial two meetings, and I parried each time by pointing out that I didn't know enough yet (we hadn't reached conceptual agreement). Her continual gentle pressure was met by my continual but firm resistance.

Finally, I had gathered enough information and commitment to put together a proposal. The buyer again inquired about fees, and I said that she would have my proposal, options, and fees within forty-eight hours.

On a whim, I then said, "You've been very curious about the fees. Is there a budget you want me to stay within, so that I can formulate my proposal accordingly?"

"Well, yes," she admitted. "We've only allocated $150,000 for this project."

My estimate was that my options were going to range from $75,000 to about $110,000. "I'll do my best to stay within that allocation," I responded with all the calmness I could muster.

I provided improved and even more effective options at $128,000, $141,000, and $172,000. She chose the second one. She was relieved, and I was probably $31,000 to $66,000 wealthier for the commensurate increase in value.

28. *Seek Out New Economic Buyers Laterally During Your Projects.* This is part of the "springboard" from Chapter 1. The time to market is always the current time, so be on the lookout for opportunity as you are implementing. This is neither unethical nor illegal. It's simply smart business.

29. Respond to "Scope Creep" with "I'll Send a New Proposal."   Whenever the client requests work clearly outside of the objectives of your original agreement, accept it graciously *provided* that you can send a new proposal—with new objectives and new fees—to cover the additional work. Regard your original project objectives as "lines in the sand," and don't allow them to be blurred.

30. It Is Better to Do Something Pro Bono than to Do It for a Low Fee.   Don't ever be pegged as a low priced option. If there's something you're dying to do, or a cause you feel more than merits your attention, than do it for free as part of your pro bono work. Don't allow yourself to be pegged as a "cheap resource." Rule of thumb: NEVER do pro bono work for a profit-making entity.

THE THIRD FIFTEEN

31. If You Do Something for Free, Send an Invoice.   Show the pro bono client what your actual fee would have been, and then waive it, showing a net of nothing due. That way you've established your fee for that particular project in the mind of that "buyer" and of anyone else on the board, on the committee, or in the room. (*Note:* This does not constitute a "donation" or tax deductible item under current IRS rules, so don't attempt to use it as a deduction.)

32. Fees Have Nothing to Do with Supply and Demand, Only with Value. Don't listen to the "experts" who tell you that you can raise fees when demand exceeds supply, which is a formula to work harder, not smarter. You want to work smarter, not harder. Every year, ask your trusted advisors and clients to help you assess the value you're providing. You may just be the worst judge and the biggest impediment to raising your own fees.

33. Raise Fees at Least Every Two Years.   Actively and aggressively increase your fees for the same kind of value you've provided in the past about every two years or so. Your customers, clients, and suppliers are doing the same. Even in low inflation times, other expenses mount. If you have occasional base fees you use—for a keynote speech or strategy retreat, for example—raise this by at least 10 percent every two years.

34. If You Are Unaware of Current Market Fee Ranges, You Are Undercharging. When you network and talk casually to clients, try to find out what the general ranges are for a variety of projects. This kind of market intelligence will help you implement your strategy, whether you choose to be the Cadillac of the market or the Taurus. Just don't choose to be the Yugo.

35. Keep Acutely Sensitive to Margins. It's not what you *make*, it's what you *keep* that's crucial. You may actually be increasing your fees while increasing your expenses at a faster clip. (This tends to happen as we become flush and invest more in marketing and client acquisition.) Analyze how much you are *keeping* and adjust your fees or your expenses accordingly to maximize margins.

36. Psychologically, Higher Fees Create Higher Value in the Buyer's Perception. I call this one "The Mercedes-Benz Syndrome." Buyers believe they get what they pay for, which is why McKinsey, IBM, Rolex, and Ferrari don't enter into price negotiations. No one says, "This is the cheapest consultant I could find, and I'm proud to have him!" Instead they say, "This person is costing us a fortune, and we were lucky to get her, so listen up!"

37. Value Can Include Subjective as Well as Objective Measures. When an executive says to me that a given result would be "priceless" or "invaluable," I move on. That's good enough. A high level buyer's relief from stress, anxiety, unpleasant situations, a poor image, safety concerns, and similar pressures is worth a great deal. Go with that.

38. Use Other People Only when Absolutely Necessary. Use subcontractors if (a) you don't have a requisite skill; (b) you need "legs" because you can't interview all over the country on the same day; or (c) you're bored with the nature of the work. But don't use them as a "show of force" or because you think it adds credibility. What it does in decrease profit, no matter how much you've boosted the revenue line.

The higher level your buyer, the more you can afford to include subjective measures and the buyer's personal metrics. The lower level the buyer, the more you must seek quantifiable measures and commit them to writing.

39. Introduce New Value to Existing Clients to Raise Fees in These Accounts. Suggest that a client consider using the traditional customer and employee surveys as a device to get customers together with employees who never otherwise see them to create a greater sense of accountability. Offer to combine the annual performance evaluation process directly with the periodic succession planning system. Don't simply sit back and do the same thing every year.

40. Do Not Accept Referral Business on the Same Basis as the Referring Source. A colleague might refer business to you from a client where the colleague is paid by the hour or day. Don't accept the same terms. Immediately educate the buyer that you and your colleague work differently, and your arrangements will be somewhat different. This will protect your fee ranges, avoid your having to refuse the work, and prevent you from being branded as a per diem consultant.

41. Ask the Comparison Question. When a prospect says, "That's more than we intended to spend" or "We never imagined it would cost that much," point to a copy machine or computer and ask, "What's your annual cost for warranties on this equipment? It's more than the sum total of this project. Are you really so willing to invest more in preventive maintenance than you are in human development?" (Or make whatever case it is that benefits your project.) Do some homework and create these comparisons in advance—you can use ruined postage, cafeteria subsidies, carpet cleaning, etc. It works wonderfully for putting your fees into perspective.

42. *When Forced into Phases, Offer Partial Rebates to Guarantee Future Business.* When the client insists on a phased approach to a complex project (for example, needs analysis, design, pilot, implementation, monitoring, etc.) that the client won't buy into all at once, then offer a rebate from the fee for the prior phase on the succeeding one if the buyer commits before the prior phase is completed. This tends to dissuade buyers from looking for alternatives at every new phase, using your work from the prior phase.

43. *Cite a Time Frame for the Proposal's Acceptance.* Tell the buyer that the fees—and any discounts you may be offering for one-time payment, for example—can be honored for thirty days, after which a new proposal will be required. After all, you have the right to manage your business and your time investment, and the client can't suddenly determine, ninety days from now, that you should proceed full steam ahead. Force the client to make a decision within a reasonable time if his or her investment is to be protected.

44. *At Least Every Two Years, Consider Jettisoning the Bottom 15 Percent.* All of us are burdened by business that made sense at one time but not now, business that is accustomed to too much service for too little money, and business that is comfortable but unchallenging. We can't reach out unless we let go, and we must let go of non-productive, low-potential business. I've seen large firms dragged down by these anchors. Refer the business to someone who will appreciate it and handle it even better than you.

45. *At Year-End, Always Emphasize Early Payment.* Clients will often have "money to burn" in the fourth quarter of their fiscal year, which is returned to the corporate coffers if unused. Make it clear that your accounting system allows for advance payments in current fiscal years to be applied to future business. This is an ideal way for a client to utilize budget for next year's work, thereby improving next year's margins (a return but no expense). Remember that some clients operate on fiscal years that are different from the calendar year, and you should find that out very early.

THE FINAL FIFTEEN

46. Practice Saying, "I Can Do That for You."   When a buyer trusts you, he or she will often remark about things that have to be accomplished outside of your project. This might be a facilitator for a strategy retreat, a mediator in an acquisition, or a presenter for an awards dinner. If the need matches your competencies, then casually suggest you could do it if needed. But don't do it for free. As always, provide the buyer with some options. Often, the buyer won't realize that you are multi-faceted.

47. Start with Payment Terms Maximally Beneficial to You Every Time.   For example, explain that your policy is full fee in advance. If the client finds that unacceptable, then offer 50 percent on acceptance, and 50 percent in forty-five days (no matter what the length of the project). But if you start with nothing down, and gradual payments, I can guarantee that you'll wind up searching for your fees well after the project is over, which means you've received much less money than someone else getting the same fee paid in advance. Beneficial terms to you equal higher profits.

48. Suggest Key Objectives Beyond the Project.   One of my buyers began talking to his own staff about how to utilize my help in the next year, well beyond the current retainer. I realized that I had offered sufficient inducement to have him think long-term. Don't be blatantly self-promotional. Simply suggest that "Here are three things to accomplish next year that would exploit current successes still more" or "You're not in a position to assign some resources against this new market in the months ahead."

49. If Payments Are Late, Pursue the Buyer.   Don't fool around in accounts payable if a scheduled payment or expense reimbursement isn't received. Immediately go to the buyer and state, "We have a small problem." The buyer will always be in a better position to expedite things internally than will you from the outside. Consider this a joint problem, not your personal misfortune.

A participant in my mentor program was having a very tough time raising fees for his sales skills workshops and training. We had practiced all of the right moves, all of the rebuttals, and all of the value propositions.

Then I noticed that he had in his briefcase a set of promotional materials that I had never seen. "Oh," he said, "I didn't want to bother you with this. It's just the stuff I send out to initial inquiries."

As I glanced through it, I found a fee schedule based on type of workshop and days. He had forgotten that it was in there.

Check your materials, web pages, and all other promotional sources to ensure that you are not inadvertently providing a constricted payment schedule.

---

50. Offer Incentives for One-Time, Full Payments.   You never know until you ask. By offering a modest (5 to 10 percent) discount for payment on acceptance, you just may put a six-figure check in the bank tomorrow. *Note:* Some organizations have rules in their accounts payable departments that any accepted proposal or contract that offers a discount mechanism must be accepted with the discount.

51. Be Clear on What the Client Owes for Expenses.   I had created a $3,500 slide presentation for a sophisticated workshop based on my consulting results before it dawned on me that the client was responsible for that expense. I'm glad I had the breakthrough before the project ended! If you've created something uniquely required for that client and not simply utilized your generic materials or equipment, the chances are that it might be reimbursable.

52. Send in Expense Reimbursement Requests Promptly.   I actually had to counsel a consultant with dreadful cash flow problems who had nearly $100,000 in outstanding expense reimbursements unsubmitted going back over a year. Send these in every single month, and never agree to a period longer than a month. If you don't like detail, too bad—I don't like wasting time at the dentist, but I prefer that to my teeth rotting. Hire a bookkeeper by the hour if you must, but send these in religiously, with receipts, to avoid questions and delay.

53. Read the Fine Print, then Push Back.   Many clients will have a generic contract sent to you *accompanying their approval to begin the project per your proposal.* The problem is that the contract will often supercede your proposal by demanding the right to cancel on short notice, pay expenses within 120 days, and creating other conditions beneficial only to the client. Read the fine print and respond to your buyer (not the purchasing people or the legal department, who may have sent the offensive document). Tell the client that the two of you have just a few unexpected conflicts to work out. At worst, you can probably compromise on the most odious parts.

54. Never Accept Payment Subject to Conditions to Be Met on Completion. Conditions change. Buyers get hit by beer trucks. The project is never quire "finished." If you allow yourself to fall into this trap, you deserve what you get (or what you don't get). You don't buy an oven with the agreement that you'll finish paying after it has cooked its last meal. Don't allow yourself to be fried in this dilemma.

Manual laborers get paid when their work is done, knowledge workers when the work is beginning. You don't pay for a book after you've completed reading it, and you don't pay for software after you've mastered it. You're not even paying the car manufacturer or house builder over time, but the bank. Do you really want to be in the loan business?

55. Focus on Improvement, Not on Problem Solving.   Everyone can solve problems, and problem solving is a commodity. But few people can systematically "raise the bar" and improve performance of already stellar operations. Yet that's where the value is. It's a question of the all-stars improving still further. Orient yourself to innovation, not problem solving, and the worth of your project will be commensurately higher.

56. Have the Client Absorb Expense Billing.   Explore whether the client will establish a master bill at a frequently used hotel, provide tickets through the client's travel agent, and provide limo service for local pick-up. Many clients will, and an administrative assistant can take care of everything. Not only does this help cash flow by preventing payments and waits for reimbursement, but it also reduces the number of invoices a client sees and reduces the total costs associated with your project (since the expense amounts are usually absorbed within corporate accounts). Consequently, you improve your cash flow, and you look better, as well.

57. Provide Proactive Ideas, Benchmarking, Best Practices from Experience. Don't become "industry bound." Demonstrate value to the buyer by bringing to bear experiences in other industries and in other conditions that can contribute to improving the current client's condition. Allow your "weaknesses" to actually be your strengths.

58. Cite U.S. Dollars Drawn on U.S. Banks.   If you are an American based in the U.S., whenever you propose any overseas business—even for a U.S. company—stress that all funds are to be paid in U.S. dollars drawn on U.S. banks and that your fees are quoted in U.S. dollars. If you don't, not only will the currency translation hurt you severely, but U.S. banks often charge as much as 25 percent to convert foreign checks issued in non-U.S. funds.

59. Practice Stating and Explaining Your Fees.   Practice your responses so that you're neither sweating profusely nor losing eye contact. Like a basketball player who bounces the ball three times before every foul shot to get into a "routine" or a baseball batter who take five practice swings, you need to get into a "groove" that allows you to conversationally say, "It's $75,000. Can we proceed?"

60. *Always Be Prepared to Walk Away from Business.* Few devices will raise fees as much as this one. Never be anxious. If you're at an impasse, simply say, "I've enjoyed meeting with you, but I don't think I can undertake the project given what you're offering. Let's stay in touch." Often, you'll be stopped before you're even out of your chair. But just as the client can say "no," so can you. Don't be afraid to reject business that's not in the form most advantageous for you.

CHAPTER 7 ROI

- Maximizing your profits means improving the top line *and* controlling the expense line. What you *keep,* not what you make, is the key.
- Use the guidelines above as a template that you can apply to your business on a periodic basis. There will always be room for improvement, because none of us do all sixty things equally well or apply them uniformly. If you have a staff, use this as a conversation point at meetings and strategy sessions.
- We control much more of the profit dynamic than we think we do, but the way we educate the buyer, insist on our rights, and have the confidence to forge our own policies will determine how successful we are at protecting our bottom lines.

If you can't find several ways to increase profits from sixty suggestions for raising fees, then you aren't interested. If you haven't highlighted and noted at least a few of the options, then you may just be reading and not learning, which is never enough.

How to Prevent and Rebut Fee Objections

Since You've Heard Them All Before, How Can You Not Know the Answers?

I'm constantly aghast at salespeople who wring their hands, rend their garments, and give up the fight when a prospect reacts with the quite normal reaction of, "I don't think I need that." If you've been in the sales arena for longer than a month and *haven't* heard every imaginable objection, then you've been embedded under a rock.

We, as consultants, know what our prospects' objections are going to be. There is no excuse not to be prepared for them. That doesn't mean that we'll be able to convert every single contact into a sale, but it does mean that we should be able to engage the buyer in a more prolonged dialogue and provide ourselves with more opportunities with the decision maker to influence his or her ultimate choice.[1]

There is a succession of "filters" (see Figure 8. 1) that we must negotiate to achieve a positive buying decision. Some require "footwork" and maneuvering, such as getting through or circumventing feasibility buyers and committees to reach the economic buyer. Some require careful questioning and discerning listening in order to reach conceptual agreement.

But one of the most critical and most, well, bungled, steps is dealing with early buyer resistance in the form of quite natural objections and rejections of the consultant's value or potential impact. The reasons include:

- We tend to take rejection personally and strive to avoid placing ourselves in a position of possible rejection
- We provide a "sales spiel" or other selling retort instead of a true response to the buyer's real objections
- We don't recognize the generic nature of the objection and offer rebuttals that address our comfort areas and not the client's *dis*comfort areas

> It makes as much sense to ignore the buyer's discomfort to focus on our own areas of comfort in rebutting objections as it does to search for lost keys in areas of good light even if we lost the keys in the shadows.

THE FOUR FUNDAMENTAL AREAS OF RESISTANCE

There is a wonderful, apocryphal story of a man encountering a friend on the street, searching the ground under a street light. "What are you doing," asks the man.

---

[1]Once again, I must emphasize that this chapter and its techniques apply only when dealing with the economic buyer.

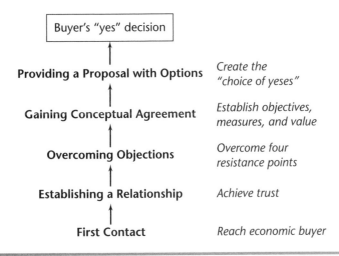

```
            ┌──────────────────────┐
            │ Buyer's "yes" decision │
            └──────────────────────┘
                       ↑
   Providing a Proposal with Options    Create the
                                        "choice of yeses"
                       ↑
     Gaining Conceptual Agreement       Establish objectives,
                                        measures, and value
                       ↑
        Overcoming Objections           Overcome four
                                        resistance points
                       ↑
     Establishing a Relationship        Achieve trust
                       ↑
            First Contact               Reach economic buyer
```

Figure 8.1. Filters to Be Overcome to Reach a Buying Decision

"I'm looking for my lost car keys," responds the friend.

"How did you happen to lose them here?"

"Oh, I didn't lose them here. I think I lost them a block away when I entered the restaurant."

"Then why are you searching here?"

"The light is better here."

It doesn't matter where your "light" is better when you're trying to find the reasons for the buyer's resistance. What matters is where the buyer actually lost your reasoning and value.

There are four major, generic areas of prospect resistance and potential objection. We know what they are.[2] We might as well get good at responding to them.

Resistance Point #1: I Don't Trust You

Perhaps the most common and fundamentally understandable resistance is that the buyer has no reason to trust the consultant. The credentials might not be

---

[2] The origins of these four areas are murky, and many people take credit. I first heard them from Larry Wilson, the founder of Wilson Learning, in the early 1970s. His collaborator, I believe, was Dr. David Merrill.

strong, the route of entry might be problematic (for example, direct mail or cold call), or the consultant might have other traits that undermine credibility: poor appearance, lack of maturity, poor vocabulary, inadequate promotional materials, and so on.

I don't trust people who call me on the phone at night to try to sell me securities. I do trust my accounting firm, which was referred to me by a trusted third party, and which carefully considered whether we were right for each other. I've been with them for fifteen years and have referred other potential clients to them.

This is the primary reason that I've advocated a marketing "gravity"[3] for all consultants, so that they are known to potential clients, are referred by current clients, and possess an inherent level of trust from a cohesive body of work in the field. Not only is the creation of a name, brand, and repute a quick route to establishing trust with *any* potential buyer, but it also considerably shortcuts the process of negotiating the various "filters" between consultant and potential buyer.

When the buyer has no inherent trust—and it's important to understand that this is not *created* by something the consultant does, but rather is the *default* position unless you actively change it—it is folly to provide "benefits" about money, timing, or value. The client won't listen. And it's impossible to reach conceptual agreement without trust.

Resistance Point #2: I Don't Need You

This obstacle means that the prospect may very well trust you and even like you, but there doesn't appear to the buyer to be any need. That might mean that the prospect doesn't see anything requiring "fixing" or improvement. This is the most common plight of consultants who are merely introduced to a buyer without any specific reason other than "You two should spend some time together." A friendly buyer does that based on the advice of a third party, but sees no intrinsic need to be filled by the consultant.

This is also why so many consultants have come to me with the same fundamental question: "What do I say after I've said 'hello'?" They've managed to meet a buyer, but haven't managed to move the buyer. In fact, many people

---

[3]See the first book of this series, *The Ultimate Consultant*, and *How to Market, Establish a Brand, and Sell Professional Services* (Kennedy Information) for details on creating marketing gravity.

who don't understand these dynamics make statements such as, "I can't understand it—we get along fine, but he doesn't seem to want to hire me!"

> It's not the buyer's job to tell you about "needs." In well-run organizations, there might not be pressing issues. It's the consultant's job to demonstrate need in *improving* the client's condition though new and better performance.

Of course not. There is no perceived need. If there is no need, working on greater trust doesn't help. It's incumbent on consultants *not to* launch arbitrary torpedoes of methodology, technique, approaches, and alternatives, hoping to hit a moving target. It's far better to listen carefully and to ask precise, prompting questions to discover need (see Appendix B), to suggest need, and to create need.[4]

This phenomenon is why I've strongly suggested that the major value of consultants is to *raise the bar* to new heights, and not just "fix" problems. Even the best of organizations can steadily improve; thus there is always need that can be created, even if there is nothing obvious to be "fixed."

Resistance Point #3: I Don't Feel Any Urgency

This is the near-legendary "the timing isn't right." Every consultant has had "hot" prospects whom they could have closed immediately if only the timing had been better. And many of those consultants keep those prospects on their forecasts—or, worse, actually spend the money they're anticipating from the project—for quite a long time.

But the timing never gets better.

If a client doesn't feel a sense of urgency, then enhancing trust levels or heightening need isn't the logical response. After all, I may like you, believe in

---

[4]No one "needed" frequent flyer programs, global positioning systems, or drive-through banking and burgers, but we certainly need them today. A luxury becomes a necessity after just one successful use!

the fact that we have room to improve, or have a condition that needs remediation. But I've lived with this condition for a long time and I don't see why I have to do anything (that is, spend money) at this juncture.

Prospects typically resort to "no urgency" or "poor timing" when:

- They are afraid of disrupting the organization ("Let's leave well enough alone.")
- The return doesn't justify the investment ("I can't see justifying that expense until the problem is costing us far more than it is.")
- The perception is that everyone has to put up with this, and the prospect is not unique ("This is a 'necessary evil' which would be impossible to change.")

In this general resistance area, the consultant must create urgency. This can be accomplished by:

- Pointing out competitive actions that will threaten the client
- Identifying a unique and limited window of opportunity to address the issue
- Showing that the prospect is incurring far more damage than perceived
- Demonstrating a far greater return on investment than the prospect believed possible
- Showing that the prospect is not on a "plateau" but that the condition is actually causing a decline that is increasing in its degree and speed

When prospects tell me "the timing isn't right," I tell them the timing is *never* going to be "right." There is no ideal time to intervene in most organizations. So what's the real nature of the reluctance?

Resistance Point #4: I Don't Have the Money to Pay You

This is the most commonly cited rejection by consultants, and it's mistakenly assumed as the primary objection of most buyers. It is not.

If you've been reading carefully to this point, you've probably come to agree that most resistance is not about money: It's about trust, need, and urgency. If there is trust, and perceived need, and sufficient urgency, *money can almost always be found.* After all, few buyers wake up in the morning and say, "What a beautiful day. I wonder if I can hire Alan Weiss?" And few budgets contain discretionary funds for consultants to be hired for concerns unanticipated, unappreciated, and unheard of.

Most consulting "budgets" must be found and created, meaning that the money originates in other areas. It is "taken" or appropriated from other budgets and other sources. There is *never* any money, in the sense of quickly available, earmarked funds for consultants.

So the money objection is the easiest, most common, and most misunderstood. It is almost always an excuse, and a "cover up" for one of the first three areas not being satisfied. Yet consultants, upon hearing "I'd love to, but we have no budget," quietly and complacently fold up their tents, leave their cards, mutter "Let's keep in touch," and disappear into the night.

It's time to have some backbone and buy some floodlights. When a client does say, "We need to do this and I want you to do it for us, but I don't have budget," then the consultant can help the client find the funds. When the first three needs (or possible objections) have truly been addressed, then the client and consultant can collaborate on how to find funds and payment terms that are mutually satisfactory (for example, pay one-half in this fiscal year, one-half in next; or provide stock as partial compensation; or take the funds from the annual convention budget and hold the meeting within the country and not overseas).

We're going to discuss below some techniques to counter specific points of objection and demurral, but keep them in the context of the four major areas above. Your approach should be determined by which of these areas is causing the buyer's resistance at any given time. There may be occasions when all four are working against you, but that is relatively rare. The probability is that one or perhaps two are most on the buyer's mind, and that the fourth—no money— is rarely an objection in actuality (although it may be the one verbalized).

If a prospect admits to need, trusts you as a professional and competent resource, and believes the time is right to act, the money will be found. Consequently, the budget is always the worst place to start, because it derails the conversation from the actual and pivotal reasons for the client's rejection.

And worse, focusing on the budget prompts the consultant to lower fees, rather than address the true issues behind the resistance. If that's not a double whammy, I don't know what is.

MAINTAINING THE FOCUS ON VALUE

Here's an ironclad rule: If you're in a discussion about fees and not value, then you've lost control of the discussion. Prospects often want to go immediately to a discussion of costs. It's important to understand the psychology of this tropism. The buyer wants to deal with fees—costs—early because they provide the easiest excuse for him or her to be rid of you. You're not dealing with a real objection, but actually with a very effective technique (if not correctly countered) to immediately end further discussion.

The rebuttal to this immediate discussion of fees is not to do it. Once you agree to talk about fees, you have enabled and empowered the prospect to focus on the cost side of the equation, not the outcome or value side.[5] If you become a willing accomplice to this tactic, you might as well leave your card and disappear into the night. It ain't going to get better.

Here are the major rebuttals to use when the prospect immediately wants to know what you charge:

- "I don't know what the fees would be, since I don't know what you need or even if I'm the right consultant. Can we spend some time talking about your situation first? And then I'll be in a better position to answer that question."
- "It would be unfair to you to even attempt a response. We've just met, and both of us need to explore and learn a few things first. Let's table that issue until I can provide a thoughtful proposal, which won't take long if I can ask you a few questions now."
- "Actually, it would be unethical for me to give you any response. I don't know what you need, or whether I have the competency to respond to those needs. Let's explore those areas, and then we can talk about value and investment at the appropriate time."
- "The range will be from $5,000 to $1,000,000. Seriously, I have no idea. Let's explore what's involved and see whether a relationship even makes sense for both of us. If it does, I'm sure we'll find some mutually beneficial way to work together."

---

[5]See Figure 1.3 in Chapter 1.

- "What's your budget? [The prospect doesn't know or won't say.] Of course you can't say, and neither can I. We both need to learn more if we're going to have a responsible and cost-effective solution to the issue. So let's begin with what you're trying to accomplish."

The prospect can't discuss fees if you refuse to do so. No prospect that I've ever met has ended the conversation at that point. This dynamic is controlled by the consultant, not the buyer. But the consultant usually surrenders the field as soon as the dreaded "How much do you charge?" is uttered.

The key for the consultant is to sidestep this issue using one of the rebuttals, or a combination of rebuttals, demonstrated above. Under no circumstances should you agree to discuss fees prior to:

- Meeting the economic buyer
- A trusting relationship being formed
- The four generic resistance factors being overcome
- Agreement on objectives, measures, and value
- Agreement to entertain a written proposal with a "choice of yeses"

That might sound like a long time to "hold out," but believe me, it's the *refusal* to cite fees that will lead to higher fees.

Alan's fourth theorem of fee dynamics: The earlier a fee is quoted, the lower the ultimate fee will be; the later a set of fees is quoted, the higher they will be.

Corollary: When a set of fees is quoted at the ideal moment in the sales process, the buyer will tend to migrate up the set to the higher fees in return for perceived higher value.

BORING IN ON THE SUBJECT

It's embarrassingly common for a consultant to negotiate all the shoals and rapids of project negotiations and arrive at the proposal stage only to find the buyer with a near-fatal case of "sticker shock." That occurs when the client, despite having stipulated to several millions of dollars of savings and improvement in the project results, and believing in the consultant's ability to achieve them, also believes—quite seriously—that the fee will be around $5,000, while the consultant's most inexpensive option—believed to be a "good deal" by the consultant—is $55,000.

How can this happen so far into the discussions and after conceptual agreement? The cause is two-fold:

1. Some consultants fail to develop a "sense" about the client's philosophy of return on investment and overall spending.
2. Some clients are totally out of touch with investment needs.

The reasons for the second condition are these (which you can use as "red flags" should you want to test for willingness to invest early):

- Never used consultants in the past; totally unfamiliar with investing in external help
- Used very inexpensive and inexperienced consultants in the past, which has caused an incorrect "education" and precedent
- Tight cost controls and a zealous focus on the expense side of the business; doesn't see ROI, only costs
- Overwhelming focus on the short term
- Losing money and business in desperate straits
- Small business owner is weighing personal and business expense needs
- Sees the consultant as "new" or not totally credible, feels that consultant is getting a chance to prove herself, so fee can be commensurately low

Some clients are hard to read. Others are deliberately deceptive. When you're the least bit uncertain, find out what the budget is. You won't be killed, but you might be shocked.

When these signs are present, you need to ascertain what the buyer's budget expectations are. Don't forget: Few buyers have "set aside" consultant funding, so the money has to be "found" somewhere. And if you're in reason number 1 above as well—you're not skilled in determining the budget conversationally—then you must find out formally.

Here's how to do that. *After* conceptual agreement is reached but *before* the proposal is even created, ask the buyer a variation of the following question:

> "You've been very kind and I'm in a position to offer a proposal with some investment options for you. Since there are options for achieving these goals, is there a budget amount you'd like me to stay within?"

Another approach:

> "We've made fine progress, and I don't want to waste your time or mine as we go forward. Is there a budget—or even a rough amount in your mind—that represents the limit of your investment in this project?"

And one more, which I call the New York (direct) approach:

> "We're ready to move to a proposal but, before we do, my experience has shown that it's important to understand any constraints on our approach. What is the budget you've allocated, now that we've reached this level of agreement?"

My suggestion is to ask these questions *after* conceptual agreement, because you will have the best chance to convince the buyer that a significant investment is justified at that point. But do it *before* the proposal so that you don't waste your time if the buyer's expectations are simply ridiculous.

There are three responses to my questions above, and they, in turn, deserve certain reactions from you:

Response #1. "What is this, the 'wedding reception' approach, and the more money I have, the better the reception? I don't want to disclose what I'm prepared to spend." This usually indicates you don't have a very trusting relationship. You should respond: "I've come to respect you and don't want to waste your time. My judgment at this point is that the investment range is going to be

$35,000 to $65,000, depending on how much certainty you're seeking. Is that in the ballpark?"

If the client tells you to go ahead, then you've prepared the buyer and there can't be "sticker shock." If the buyer says the range is too high, then part as friends.

Response #2. "Our expectation is that the project should cost somewhere around $20,000." If that's realistic, then respond, "We can work within that, and I'll get the proposal to you tomorrow." If it's unrealistic, then reply, "I don't think we can do it for that amount. We're probably talking about $35,000 at the low end to $65,000 at the high end. Do you want to discuss this further?"

This allows for total honesty. The client might say, "Okay, I'm prepared for a slightly worse case, go ahead." If not, then part friends.

> Note that any discussion of budget at this point is always based on the investment, since the objectives and their values are already established. This is far superior to discussing fees at the outset, when they are simply isolated costs.

Response #3. "We're willing to spend whatever is reasonable to make this happen." The response here should be, "Thanks, I'm sure you'll find the investment well within reason in view of the benefits we've already detailed. The proposal will be here tomorrow."

Asking about the budget is perfectly fine, providing you do it at the right time and are prepared for the three categories of response. Here are the conditions:

- You have been talking to the economic buyer all along
- You have achieved conceptual agreement with the economic buyer
- You are uncertain of the buyer's understanding of the level of investment required

A brief digression: If you are speaking professionally in addition to your consulting, and a prospective buyer asks about your appearing at an event, ask very early what the budget is. Many infrequent or novice buyers of speaking services have no idea about fees, which vary tremendously in the field.

OFFERING REBATES

I offer rebates under certain circumstances, and I'm not talking about returning a coupon or buying a special appliance. I offer rebates when I find that the project calls for phases (not options, which I always provide) and I want to encourage the client to utilize my help through all of the phases. A phase is a timed step or sequence, each succeeding one dependent on the successful completion of the prior one. Typically, a project might require an information gathering phase, then recommendations for intervention, then creation of the interventions, then the implementation, and then follow-up and monitoring. While I'd prefer to include all phases in one project, it's sometimes impossible to do so, since you can't predict needs further down the line until earlier steps are completed.

In this case, I suggest offering the client another form of a "good deal." Offer the client the "rebate" of a percentage of the phase 1 fee if you're hired for phase 2, and so on down the line. What's the right percentage? Who knows? But I keep it to 50 percent or below. (The higher the fee for phase 2, the higher the percentage rebate—don't make the mistake of looking at the fee for phase 1 for the rebate percentage!)

Example: The client has agreed to a phase 1 needs analysis among customers for a $35,000 fee. The second phase would be the development of a better customer response system, based on the customer feedback and priorities. You're estimating that phase 2 would be in the range of $125,000 to $175,000. You tell the client that, should you be chosen to implement phase 2 of the project, you will rebate 50 percent of the phase 1 fee. That means that you're still netting $90,000 to $140,000 on phase 2, while greatly reducing the chances of another consultant being brought in or the client deciding to do it internally.

Of course, if you think that you're a "lock" for the continuing phases, there's no need to offer a rebate, or you can offer just a token one. But I always like to think of "the fourth sale first," so I believe rebates are a good idea in these situations, *particularly with new clients with whom you don't have a track record.* If you think of the totality of the several phases as the real project, then the rebates can be reasonable reductions against the very large total investment.

> Don't give rebates unless phases are in the best interests of the project and the client. When they are, offer the potential rebate in the proposal itself so that it's committed to writing in the same document which the client is accepting as the basis for phase 1 work.

You might want to change the name to "discount" or "professional courtesy." I've had no trouble with "rebate," but you might be more fastidious. The key is, it's a tool to be used when appropriate. I find that I tend to offer them relatively rarely, but with great effect when I do.

UTILIZING "SMACK TO THE HEAD" COMPARISONS

There are times when the client will balk at a fee, even when you know darn well that the fee is entirely reasonable and the "good deal" is terrific. You'll also be certain that the buyer can afford it, and the reluctance will sometimes start to get on your nerves. This often happens *after* a proposal has been presented, and you believed that all such contingencies were long since dealt with.

You'll be very frustrated. So the answer is to get a metaphorical large board and smack the buyer upside the head. Here's how you do that. Find comparisons that will embarrass the buyer into giving up his or her resistance. Some buyers are simply maneuvering for a deal; some have an ego that won't be sated until they get a concession; some are transferring other issues in their life (a fight with a spouse, a lost promotion) to you. No matter. Whatever the cause, don't fall for it. Fight back.

I've found the best comparisons to be the following, but any imaginative consultant can easily add to my list (in fact, it's fun):

- Point out that the client is spending more on copy machine warranties and repair than the total cost of your proposal
- Demonstrate that spillage and ruined product costs ten times the proposal's most expensive option
- Ask what one lost customer a week is costing

- Ask what the cost of a very bad hire is
- Cite what the cost of each talented employee who leaves the organization is (including replacement, lost business, training, succession planning, and so on); don't skimp
- Ask what the client's most recent gaffe in a failed new office or a poorly received new product cost
- Cite what the savings would be if R&D commercialization time were cut by 25 percent
- Ask what the board of directors' reaction would be if they considered the cost of the current problems versus the unwillingness to make this investment in their elimination

You get the idea. Have these ready, because you never know when you'll need them. The most agreeable and friendly client can "spring" an unexpected fee objection, even after conceptual agreement and receipt of the proposal. It's your fault if you're not prepared.

> Most embarrassing comparisons will hold true from organization to organization, so the preparation of a few "beauts" will serve you reliably over the course of time.

There are several sources to use to develop your "smacks upside the head":

1. In your preliminary discussions leading up to conceptual agreement, make some gentle inquiries into the costs the prospective client is incurring in some of these areas. Listen for voluntary disclosures (for example, "Do you know we're spending $175,000 just on software 'fixes'?").
2. Use the Internet search engines to turn up statistics and facts on common issues. For example, find out about the average costs of turnover, lawsuits, recruiting, and so on.
3. Tear relevant items out of your daily reading. *The Wall Street Journal* and *Business Week* are forever publishing information on the costs of accounting, legal, computers, and other areas.

4. Remember that many of these are generic, and you can use them from client to client. Save your best ones to use in key situations. I'm forever pointing to the copy machine "culprit" sitting in a corner as an example of the client being willing to spend more money on equipment maintenance than on human development.

The embarrassing comparison will take care of most of the flimsy and capricious objections to fees. Sometimes you just have to pack a strong (metaphorical) weapon.

IGNORING THE COMPETITION

I've often stated that if you don't know what the competition is charging, you're probably undercharging. But I don't mean to imply that you should peg your fees to that of the competition. The former is merely market intelligence. The latter is simply foolhardy.

Don't allow any buyer to tell you that the competition is charging "X" and that you should come in below that. Don't listen to the argument that "here's what we've paid in the past and expect to continue to pay" for consulting services.

The whole point in developing a relationship prior to conceptual agreement is to ferret out these kinds of (sometimes) legitimate expectations and (sometimes) devious devices to depress fees. You are not like past consultants (which is why you're there) and you don't do what the competition does (which is why you're there). Telling a Mercedes dealership that the Buick place down the street charges much less will get you an uncomprehending stare or a firm "So what?" Telling an airline that you're accustomed to paying the amount of tolls on the New Jersey Turnpike to drive from New York to Philadelphia, and that you expect an equivalent air fare, will get you escorted away. Telling a theater that your budget only permits you to pay $2.50 will not gain you admittance to the show. So why should you listen to similar, irrational arguments?

Educate your buyer immediately and repeatedly that what's gone before is history, and what goes on around you is irrelevant. The only thing that matters is the "good deal": Is the client achieving a great return on a reasonable investment? You'll be happy to demonstrate that via a proposal at the appropriate time, if the buyer can cooperate with some information at the moment. But you're not interested in comparisons and arbitrary parameters.

After all, this must be a "win/win" relationship. What if you told the buyer that:

- Prior buyers paid a minimum of $600,000
- Consultants who do what you do receive an average of $450,000 per contract
- You're simply not prepared to accept anything less than $475,000, because that's your expectation

You'd be thrown off the property, probably under armed guard. But why allow the client to express equally absurd expectations?

> Reverse the client's logic about expecting low fees—that you're expecting high fees—and you'll find equally moronic lines of logic. Point that out and move on.

Don't dignify bizarre positions. Educate the buyer correctly from the outset. Ignore the competition and the competition's poor strategy. Now is the time to be your own person.

The only person deciding what your profit level is should be you. It's a mistake to allow the buyer to do that, and it's insane to allow the competition to influence it in any way at all. So stop doing that.

CHAPTER 8 ROI

- There are four fundamental resistance points: no need, no trust, no money, no urgency. You must address the correct one. Seldom do all four come into play, and "no trust" is usually the fundamental problem. "No money" is usually a red herring.
- Always focus on value, not fees; otherwise you've lost control of the discussion. Don't hesitate to ask about the buyer's intended budget, especially if certain "red flags" appear during early conversations.
- Offer rebates on multi-phase projects, when such phases are truly called for and are in the client's best interests.

- Prepare yourself with embarrassingly harsh comparisons for those times when an otherwise agreeable buyer has fee "issues" that you know should be brushed aside.
- Ignore the competition, since neither the buyer nor the competition should establish your profitability levels.
- Remember that most of the fee-setting dynamic is actually under our control and influence, and that we tend to sacrifice this strength.
- The best way to support high fees is first to believe in the value you're providing yourself, and then to convince the buyer of it.

There is no such animal as a "new" objection. We've heard them all before, every one. If the prospect has successfully rebutted your position, the buyer is simply better prepared than you are, and you haven't established a "good deal."

Setting Fees for Non-Consulting Opportunities

*How to Make Money While
You Sleep, Eat, Play, and, Well,
Make Money Elsewhere*

I've often observed that I'm constantly surprised at how stupid I was two weeks ago. Once upon a time I would say "two years ago." I'd like to think today's shorter time frame is not so much a sign of my increasing dementia as it is one of exploding opportunities in this profession.

There is nothing wrong with the position that holds that one is a consultant and not interested in the peripheral and tangential activities that may distract one from the work at hand. Fair enough. But if you're at all like me, and you believe that consulting is simply an input to a much greater end—our lives, loved ones, and legacy—then why not explore the myriad of opportunity that a successful consulting practice can generate?

Basically, there are a lot of ways to make money in the profession but, like the nature of our consulting fees, there are also a lot of ways to charge incorrectly and shortchange ourselves in terms of receiving fair compensation for our value. Just this morning, a consultant in my mentor program asked if he had a right to charge a high fee for speaking to an organization that had been attracted to him by a book he had written. "After all," he (incorrectly) reasoned, "they can get most of this out of the book, so I don't think I'm bringing much extra value."

If that's what you believe, then you're right.

If you're of the "pure" consulting philosophy, you might want to skip this chapter. On the other hand, you might want to read on and see what you're missing. And if you're a big believer in maximizing your income, especially in non-labor-intensive pursuits, then pick up your highlighter.

KEYNOTE SPEAKING: DON'T CHARGE FOR YOUR SPOKEN WORDS

The intent of this discussion is to provide help in how to set fees for speaking activities. If you're interested in *how* to begin a professional speaking career, or *how* to craft a speech and get onto the lucrative speaking circuit, see my book *Money Talks.*[1]

A keynote speech is usually forty-five to ninety minutes in length. These are general session speeches (delivered to the full assembly and not to concurrent sessions or breakout groups). Technically, only the opening speech is a true "keynote" (sounding the "key note" for the conference) and the others are plenary speeches delivered during the course of the conference.

> No one is worth very much for an hour of his or her time. As in consulting, it's the *value* that you provide that will support your speaking fee.

---

[1]*Money Talks: How to Make a Million as a Speaker* (McGraw-Hill, 1998).

The least expensive speakers delivering these speeches are paid about $3,500 by major trade associations and large organizations, and the most expensive are paid from $75,000 to $100,000. These latter people have included Colin Powell, Norman Schwarzkopf, certain athletes, and so on.[2] The typical noncelebrity, highly regarded keynote speaker is paid between $7,500 and $12,000 at this writing.

At the lower end of that scale, speaking just once a month generates $100,000 of what can be pure profit. Speaking twice a month at the higher end generates just under $300,000. Do I have your attention?

There are also more traditional training opportunities, which may involve concurrent sessions, workshops, and so on, and may take several hours or several days. I favor keynotes, since they are the least labor intensive and command the highest fees, but longer training sessions are also clearly viable options for any consultant.

In terms of your fees, I think there are three main considerations:

Factor #1: Establish Your Value

Your materials, website, conversations, and other promotional efforts should focus on value, not on topic, not on delivery, and not on methodology. Remember the value package concept from Chapter 1 (which we've repeated here as Figure 9.1)?

Your speaking approach must accentuate the client's future. The more of your past that is relevant, unique, interesting, and attractive, the more you can potentially contribute to the client's future. The intervention—the speech—is merely the transfer point.

If you can keep this process in mind, then you'll have no reluctance to charge for your worth. If you concentrate solely on the nature of your intervention (a speech, workshop, seminar, or training session), then you'll constantly wonder how you can charge more than a modest amount. And you'd be correct.

---

[2] I believe the unofficial record was set by former President George Bush when he accepted stock options to speak in Tokyo, which subsequently amounted to several million dollars for about an hour's work.

Consultant's Past	Current Intervention	Client's Future
• experiences	• coaching	• higher productivity
• education	• survey	• lower attrition
• accomplishments	• redesign	• higher morale
• development	• workshop	• improved image
• travels	• retreat	• better performance
• work history	• etc.	• greater market share
• beliefs		• greater profit
• victories/defeats		• more growth
• risks/adversity		• more innovation
• experimentation		• problems solved
		• happier customers
		• superior service

Process Flow

⎯⎯⎯⎯⎯⎯⎯⎯⎯⎯⎯⎯⎯⎯⎯⎯⎯⎯⎯⎯⟶

Figure 9.1. Value Process

Be crystal clear on the value you provide in your speeches. Educate the prospect. Do you help to improve sales, increase retention, deal with culture changes, enhance customer service, develop strategies for growth, or foster teamwork? Those are certainly more valuable objectives than "providing a speech" or "helping motivation."[3]

> The best "motivational speakers" provide pragmatic techniques for people to apply in order to improve their lives and their jobs. The worst provide empty aphorisms and "affirmations," which evanesce in the cold light of day.

[3]In fact, "motivational speakers" have a justly deserved poor reputation for froth and no substance. We had all better be motivational in our talks, but we had all better be providing solid techniques for improvement, as well.

Factor #2: Develop Options

The "choice of yeses" extends to professional speaking. For example, I can turn virtually any keynote into a solid five-figure assignment by providing options to the buyer such as these (I've made up the numbers just to provide a comparison):

- Deliver the keynote according to the buyer's objectives: $8,500
- Talk to selected participants first by phone to include their observations in the remarks and customize my approach to their issues: $2,500
- Talk to the division executives (or corporate officers, or board of directors, or trustees, etc.) to include their views, remarks, and further tailor the presentation: $3,000
- Conduct a brief survey to compare industry practices to the client's practices and highlight the distinctions: $5,000
- Appear at subsequent workout sessions with smaller groups to respond to their questions and interpret the keynote remarks down to operational concerns: $2,000
- Provide a copy of my book (or tape or other product) for every participant to bridge the remarks and their application: $1,000

You might have more and better options. But these alone add up to $22,000. Any combination will land you somewhere in the teens. And, since you're a consultant to begin with, you can provide and complete these options much better than a pure speaker, who does nothing else for a living. In other words, the options allow you to build on your innate strength.

Most speakers will not offer these options. Some buyers will tell you they can't afford them. So what? This is a sideline for you, and one that you can embark on within your own parameters. And you'd be silly not to build on the very value that you bring to the equation.

Factor #3: Use Speakers Bureaus Only on Your Terms

Bureaus are brokers between the client and the talent (you) for which they expect 25 percent of the deal (some want 30 percent and more, indicating that the government is failing in its attempts to control LSD and other hallucinatory drugs). Bureaus can be highly effective, since they bring business you would not ordinarily have acquired, and your own marketing cost is nil. However, they can be deadly and dangerous for consultants.

Bureaus will want a "fee schedule." For example, your keynote fee may be $7,500, your half-day fee may be $9,000, and your full-day fee may be $12,000. This is what they market. That's okay, *if they allow you to negotiate further with the client, providing the options suggested above.* But many bureaus won't allow you to do that out of a general paranoia, and your fees would be restricted to the $7,500 less the 25 percent commission: $5,625, net. That means that the $100,000 example above for speaking just once a month becomes $75,000, still a nice figure, but considerably lighter than it might be.

> A bureau relationship should be like a client relationship: mutually trusting, mutually beneficial, and mutually supportive. If it's not, walk away. You don't need them; they need you.

HIGHLY LEVERAGED PRACTICES FOR WORKING WITH BUREAUS

If you're going to deal with bureaus, and you're a professional consultant who is speaking, not a professional speaker who can't and doesn't consult, then follow these guidelines in your bureau relationships:

- Don't pay more than a 25 percent commission. Commissions on "spin-off" business (subsequent business generated by your appearance) should provide the same commission to the bureau for a finite period (for example, one or two years), although some bureaus reduce commission on spin-off business.
- Demand to speak to the buyer and negotiate the actual fee yourself. Bureaus almost always deal with meeting planners who are rarely economic buyers. Consequently, their demand is to conserve money, not to invest in value. After all, the higher the fee you negotiate, the higher the bureau commission.
- Develop a relationship with the bureau principal. If the two of you can't work together as peers, then walk away.

- Be clear that subsequent *consulting work* that might arise out of your speaking *is not* subject to the bureau's speaking commission. You might agree to pay 10 percent or less, but the thought of paying the bureau 25 percent of a $200,000 consulting fee is not something that is fair, justified, or sane. Make sure this is clear before you speak, since most speakers bureaus do not understand consulting at all.
- Do not invest in bureau promotional initiatives. The reason that they get 25 percent, ostensibly, is to market you. If they also insist that you pay for placement in their catalog, website, or special mailings, take a hike.
- Do not allow any money to be held in escrow. When the client pays the (typically) 50 percent deposit to hold the date, then the bureau should keep half (the commission) and send half to you. The final 50 percent should be paid directly to you no later than the presentation date itself. Any other arrangement is simply unfair to you.

The most desirable professional speaking will come directly to you (avoiding bureau fees) via your normal marketing "gravity." (I speak about fifty times a year, which is the rate I've sought to maintain, with only five or six assignments coming from bureaus.) That requires that you educate prospects about your availability as a speaker in your promotional materials, website, articles, networking, and so on. You will always be more valuable as a consultant who speaks than as a speaker who consults.

Keep your fees high. This is not your main source of income, and people believe they get what they pay for. The more unique you are as a consultant (book published, international work, media interviews, and so forth), the more valuable you are as a speaker. Finally, like consulting, speaking is about marketing, not methodology. You can always improve your platform techniques (and there are only 57,000 coaches who will be happy to help you), but unless you market you'll be speaking to yourself.

PRODUCTS

One of the biggest errors I made when I first published *Million Dollar Consulting* in 1992 was to advise that products should wait until the consultant has a firmly established repute. Actually, products can help branding and the creation of that repute.

However, since I'm talking here primarily to successful consultants, products are an important part of the repertoire in any case. And they possess the wonderful attribute of providing income while also promoting your consulting.

> The buyer said to me while walking out of the room, "By the way, can you send along four hundred copies of your book with an invoice?" I managed to say "Yes, sure," before I realized that I didn't know which book the buyer wanted.

Here is a brief description of some of the product options available to successful, innovative, and aggressive consultants.

Commercially Published Books

You can buy your books at a discount *not from the publisher* (who offers about 40 percent off), but rather from one of the book wholesalers, such as Ingram.[4] In this way, you can qualify for more than 40 percent off, get another 2 percent off for prompt payment, *and* generate royalties for yourself (since the wholesaler buys from your publisher). If your hard-cover book retails for $30, you can net $12 to $15 on your own sales using this route. (Always sell at full retail.)

Self-Published Books

This is where the serious money resides, but two factors are absolutely critical: First, the book must be good. Most self-published books are terrible, and they look as though they were produced by someone who can't even use a computer properly. Second, they should be expensive, not inexpensive. While I have some booklets that sell for $7, they are also used as free marketing vehicles when necessary. However, my large margins come from books that sell for $75 to $150. Value-based pricing can apply to books (as you've probably understood when paying for one

---

[4]Ingram Book Company, Box 277616, Atlanta, GA 30384–7616 (615/793–5000).

of those large, gaudy "coffee table" editions). You can self-publish a hard-cover book with an initial print run of two thousand copies for about $8,000, and subsequent press runs will cost about half of that. That means that you're making about $25 for a $30 book. You're better off with low volume, high margin than high volume low margin, since you're not in the book fulfillment business.

Audiocassette Tapes and Albums

Plan some of your speeches with the intent that they will be recorded for a possible product offering. (In other words, don't use the client's name repeatedly, don't cite the date, refrain from using contemporary but transient examples.) You can offer the client free copies if you need cooperation. Record the audience reaction as well with careful microphone placement.[5] These single cassettes are ideal marketing devices as well as potential products. Keep each side to about thirty minutes, which is "drive time" for a commuter. Edit them with professional introductions, elimination of "dead spots," and so on. They cost about a dollar apiece to duplicate. However, once you have several on related topics, you have a four- or six- or eight-cassette album, which you can accompany with a workbook, set of pamphlets, or manual, and a product emerges that can sell for $150 or so. Don't record tapes in a studio. They are stilted and demand perfection. Those taped "live" are more fun, more energetic, and are forgiving of errors since they are live.

Videotapes and Albums

I've found that video is less desired than audio, which is less desired than print. However, video can provide a nice augment to your product offerings, costs only about $10 for duplication, and can be created during your normal speaking endeavors. Sometimes the client will do this for the client's own purposes, and you can get a master by waiving any fee for agreeing to the arrangement.[6]

---

[5]Hire a professional recording firm. They'll charge less than $500 and it will be well worth it.

[6]I always allow audio- and videotaping for free provided that I'm given two master copies with permission to use them for product purposes, so long as client name and proprietary information are removed. A professional video team can be hired for less than $2,500, using two cameras, if you prefer to do it yourself.

This, too, always needs a live audience. In addition to what you talk about, make sure your dress is conservative and doesn't betray a date or time. I sell videos on marketing, product development, and "stories I could never tell." You can combine these with audio, print, and related materials to build quite impressive—and expensive—products.

> The key to product sales is *margin.* This is not a business in which you want "loss leaders"—you're not Kmart. Moving $40,000 of product is just silly if it earns you $2,000.

OTHER STUFF

Focus on high margin, relevant materials. I've actually seen consultants sell all kinds of "tshachkas," such as T-shirts, coffee mugs, bumper stickers, paperweights, and assorted dust collectors (although speakers are far more prone toward this nonsense). However, even items such as calendars, daily planners, and project templates are suspect, because they don't command high prices and are generally not terribly practical. If you have manuals, templates, worksheets, and related guides, which have an intrinsic and immediate application, these can be valuable products. For example, a brief pamphlet or set of instructions on behavioral interviewing, assessing recommendations, rebutting the most common objections, or using PowerPoint® might be very well-received among the appropriate client groups.

The guidelines for product sales should include these six:

1. Is there sufficient margin per sale?
2. Can I sell these to both existing clients and to others who are not clients?
3. Will they also aid in my marketing plans?
4. Can they be integrated into my current and future marketing plans?
5. Can I create them cost-effectively and "kill" any eventual poor sellers cost-effectively?
6. Can I fulfill orders expeditiously and efficiently?

If you're selling products, accept credit cards and plan for lost shipments as a cost of doing business. Use an ISBN number (International Standard Book Number)[7] so that you can distribute over Amazon.com, other web sources, bookstores, and so forth. Create a user-friendly, separate section of your website just for product sales.

REMOTE CONSULTING AND ITS LUCRATIVE NATURE

You've heard me say before that there are a lot of ways to make money. I just never imagined how many there were. Actually, we're presented with them almost every day, but we fail to set fees for them because:

- We don't take the time to recognize their intrinsic worth
- We do them "naturally" and unthinkingly
- The positioning is wrong
- We think a fee is the only source of remuneration

I've never written about these elements before because they best apply to mature, successful consultants whose name, brand, stature, and positioning have created a powerful attraction. Like a bank loan that only becomes available when you're so successful you don't need it, or a speakers bureau that wants to represent you only after you've made a name for yourself on the speaking circuit, these alternative sources of income arise when you're already doing well financially.

However, you're still willing to accept the bank's line of credit and the speakers bureaus' business, so why not embrace new sources of income that can provide for retirement, kids' college tuition, vacations, charitable donations, or simply discretionary, deserved income?

---

[7]You can acquire ISBN numbers through W.W. Bowker at: http://www.bowkerlink.com/corrections/common/home.asp

> If you are providing any kind of service, help, or advice on a continuing or even periodic basis, ask yourself, "Why aren't I charging for this?" There will often be a completely spurious reason (or no reason at all, other than your own lassitude).

Here are some alternatives for assigning fees to activities ranging from the unmistakable to the unlikely.

Remote Consulting

I once received calls all the time for "informal" help. They were sometimes from managers I had never met in non-client companies, sometimes from other consultants, and sometimes from, well, unanticipated sources (such as the person trying to patent an adhesive device I couldn't even begin to fathom, but who needed an entrepreneur's assessment of whether he was receiving competent legal help [he wasn't]). The easy problem was one of time. I could just turn these people away when I was very busy—and take time with them when I wasn't.

The tough problem was quality. Very few of these issues could be resolved (or, sometimes, even understood) within the bounds of a single phone call. My ethical quandary was whether to give incomplete advice on a quick basis, or provide more of a qualitative response at the sacrifice of still more of my time.

I decided that the best interests of the callers were served by the close attention required for a highly qualitative response, accompanied by a relationship of some duration allowing for trial and error, feedback, and further fine-tuning of the resolution.

An individual called me last week who represents the quintessential dilemma I once had but now address quite easily.

"I've read your book on speaking (*Money Talks*)," he said, "and I want you to be my mentor. I've called you determined to make this happen."

"You mean you'd like to join my formal mentor program?" I asked.

"No, money is tight. But I'm willing to work for you, help you, do whatever it takes under your terms. You haven't met anyone as determined as I am. I need to work with you to accelerate my career."

"I don't have employees, I don't need help, and my conditions are simple: You can join the program as others have in your position. That's it. No options."

"But," he yelled, "you don't know me. Give me a chance."

"That's exactly the point," I said. "I don't know you. Why should I favor you and not someone else? That's why there is an objective set of criteria for joining my program. But there are free articles, indexed, on my website, and a free newsletter. You're welcome to avail yourself of those resources."

The conversation took two minutes. I know that I helped him by not enabling his entitlement philosophy, or the mistaken notion that passion alone justifies free help. And I know I helped myself.

I've separated "remote consulting" into three areas:

Area #1: Coaching

Coaching is designed for managers and professionals working for organizations. In other words, they are not independent entrepreneurs. They usually require help with a single issue, although sometimes they are seeking longer term career advice.

My suggestion is that you provide coaching help for set intervals (for example, thirty-day periods) during which the individual can phone or email.

The meetings are never in person. Phone calls are at mutually convenient times, or on the basis of your returning the call within some satisfactory time frame (for example, twenty-four hours or less). You might choose to limit contact to no more than one phone call a week or some other standard if you wish (or provide options at different fee levels). You assess a fee for the time interval, rather than each transaction, so that the individual, in fact, has "retained" you for a limited duration and with certain restraints.

> Coaching is a very hot topic, partly due to real need and partly due to pure ego ("Of course I have my own coach"). But it's often done best on an anonymous basis and when certain situations present themselves. That's why coaching by phone and email can be so effective for the process, economical for the client, and lucrative for the consultant.

I promote the coaching option on my website so that I can refer people to it easily without long discussion. Payment is always in advance. If you were to charge even $500 for a thirty-day interval, and had three people being coached a month, that's $18,000 of pure profit derived during your "down time" that can pay the mortgage on a vacation home or tuition at a fine school. Of course, if you were to charge $1,000 and averaged four coaching clients a month, your annual profit would be $48,000, which could pay for your home mortgage or send two kids to college.

Area #2: Mentoring

I define mentoring as providing rather intimate, one-on-one assistance to other entrepreneurs. (If you were an actuary, it would be for other actuaries, or if you were a pottery maker, for other pottery makers. There has actually been a farrier in my mentoring program who has mentored other farriers.)

You might find that coaching and mentoring are similar or identical, and that's fine. But I've made the separation *for the purposes of differentiating my services and assigning proper fees for the value provided.*

As you've become more and more successful, greater numbers of people have come to you for advice. Sometimes you see yourself as "giving back to the profession," sometimes as doing a good deed, sometimes as harried, and sometimes as unfairly imposed on (see the Vignette above). No matter how great our egos, the luster of being sought out as a "star" begins to dim when people insist on free advice and intrude on our time.

Hence, mentoring. Many executive coaches have set up coaching "certification" programs. I've seen facilitators do the same, as I have people in quality control, expert witnessing, and technology consulting. I've tried to create a broad program to encompass entrepreneurs of all kinds, but about 65 percent of the participants have been consultants of one stripe or another.[8]

I also believe that mentoring takes place over a longer period of time (my program is six months). You can charge a not inconsiderable amount of money for your remote involvement, which the participant will find to be a bargain. I've tried to structure my fees so that they can be charged on a credit card and so that the client can recover them easily through higher fees and/or additional business, so that the participant can become "whole" quite quickly.

My particular program requires an investment of $3,500, payable at the outset. That's an extremely reasonable fee for my kind of high-powered help, and it hasn't been unusual for participants (who are at every level of the profession, some just beginning and some already earning in the high-six to low-seven figure range) to double and triple their income.

The key to any remote relationship is a "good deal" for both parties. I've found that the removal of a personal interaction can be more than compensated for by rapid responsiveness and adaptations to learning styles.

---

[8]We actually now have an annual mentor meeting, open to all present and past participants in the program. We've averaged over sixty people per meeting, and everyone comes at his or her own expense.

You may choose to mentor one or two people at a time, or a dozen at a time, depending on your own objectives and work schedule. But since this is truly "remote" consulting, you can always return a mentor's call or email from the road. At this writing, more than two hundred people have been through my program at $3,500 each, a fee I've kept constant from inception in 1996. I'm sure some of you are doing the math at this point.[9]

Area #4: Situational Consulting

I've been called by people for a long time who have an immediate and urgent need for help on a very clear and well-defined issue. They don't need coaching and they don't need mentoring. They just need some quick answers.

I used to do this for free, but I came to resent it. After all, I was helping people make hundreds of thousands of dollars, avoid legal problems, attract new clients, and improve their image and, often as not, they were calling on my toll-free number!

I now tell people that I can't do justice to their issue with a quick response

VIGNETTE

A guy I'll call "Roy" whom I barely knew from a professional association we both belonged to called me out of the blue. He was working on a major proposal, had heard that I was the consulting guru, and asked for my opinion about the work and his fees.

His fees were ridiculous, under $200,000, and we quickly moved them to $410,000 over two years (I'll never forget that figure). I helped him with the reasoning and how to present the proposal.

He called two weeks later to tell me he got the business. He said that something was in the mail for me. I subsequently received a gold star paperweight, with one of his aphorisms on it.

While I refrained from throwing the paperweight through my window, I didn't refrain from committing to myself that I would never provide such help for free ever again. And I haven't.

[9]People ask how I arrived at $3,500. At the time, it was the monthly payment on my Ferrari. I figured that a dozen mentorees a year would pay for the car.

to a rapidly stated quandary. I explain that there's a modest fee, in return for which we spend up to an hour on the phone (cumulatively) and exchange unlimited email for up to five business days.

If you were to charge $1,000 for this value and provide it twice a month, you'd bring in $24,000, which would pay the lease on most luxury cars. You will also, and perhaps more importantly, drive away the "energy suckers" who want to "pick your brain" until they have every last crumb consumed.

> Charging for your value, no matter how brief in duration or confined the issue, not only serves to gain pure profit, but will also drive away the parasites. Such cleansing is important in nature.

AND NOW FOR SOME PERSPECTIVE

I'm not saying that you should abandon all pro bono work or refuse to offer free assistance to anyone you please. I am saying that there's no need to give away the store, that success does not demand self-immolation, and that people realize that there is no free lunch. Or at least they should realize that, and we can help them.

You may choose not to take a personal fee, but to suggest other forms of remuneration. Here are some alternatives that I use:

- Make out the check to a favorite charity or cause
- Provide a favorable review to one of your books online
- Volunteer for a cause you are leading or backing
- Return the favor with referral business
- Return the favor by helping with some tedious work
- Participate in a sample taping you're doing for a product
- Promise to help someone else when they're ready

I'm not mercenary, but I am pragmatic. I've found that most people who seek and accept free advice seldom put a premium on it and rarely fully implement it. They know that, if they screw up or need further help, there's always more to be had for the right price: free.

Consequently, I can make a case that you're helping people more when you require that they invest—no matter how modestly—in their own success and take some accountability for implementing your help. There's nothing like paying money to force someone to analyze the return on that investment!

When we are successful, it's too easy to enable others who simply want the "short cut" version of our success without the hard work, without the dues, and without the discipline. I tell people all the time that I can't control their discipline or their talent. I've found that those who want things for free usually can't control those factors either.

One more criterion: When you are doing work that you dislike and wonder how you got "roped into it," it's time to start charging. Just as you're justified to charge more for difficult and fractious clients, you're certainly justified to charge for previously "free" work that is now driving you nuts. If the other party refuses to pay, you have ample cause to walk away. I've had to tell too many people in my life that I was helping them out of my good nature and that I didn't expect argument and debate as a result. (The people who tend to complain most bitterly in the aftermath of elections are ineluctably those who didn't bother to vote.)

There are a lot of ways to make money. You may not choose to make money doing all of them, but you owe it to yourself to at least examine them in terms of your overall life goals and business objectives. You could probably, right now, be making another $100,000 to $300,000 on your bottom line if you intelligently engaged in non-consulting activities and remote consulting.

Once a year, at least, examine your business and your talents for the potential of additional non-consulting and remote consulting income. If you don't do that, no one else will do it for you. This is a huge area for life style improvement.

CHAPTER 9 ROI

- There are a lot of ways to make money, whether for yourself or for a cause or charity that is important to you.
- In addition, charging fees for non-consulting services often provides the relief needed from those who constantly bang on your door wanting your expertise for free.
- Speaking is a primary money generator in addition to being a wonderful marketing tool. For those interested, it can be a second profession and a very lucrative source of income. But fees here, too, should be based on value and assigned over options. Training and workshops are allied endeavors.
- Products provide wonderful passive income, as well as additional branding. They, too, provide excellent marketing advantages.
- Non-consulting services and remote consulting provide as much or as little opportunity as you care to pursue. Their great power is in providing income during "down time" without travel, wear, and tear. The probability is that you're already doing a great deal of this for free, which is fine if it's a conscious choice, but deadly if it's a "necessary evil."
- The bottom line: Even a modest amount of non-consulting income can make a tremendous impact on your life goals.

Passive and remote income will keep you off airplanes and remove the burden on your retirement planning. This is because it tends to be an annuity that persists long after you elect to reduce your activities. In the trajectory of your career, you should be implementing passive income opportunities NOW.

CHAPTER 10

Fee Progression Strategies

*Why You Fall Behind
when You Stand Still*

I t's fascinating how we rigorously update our computer software, seek out the latest cell phone technology, and constantly improve our websites and press kits, but tend to ignore our fee practices as if they are fossils best left undisturbed.

This chapter is intended to provide a holistic view of fees and when and how to raise them. We've been through the tactics, the rebuttals, the options, and the preparation. Now we're going to examine the process as an ongoing strategy. Although we'll start with the early career planning to provide the continuity—and this might be of appeal to newer consultants—it's difficult to engage in a comprehensive strategy early in one's career when putting food on the table seems more important than negotiating with a client. (A closed deal of any kind is a successful negotiation!) I'm also anticipating that some sophisticated, mature, and successful people from other careers are reading this book as they enter the consulting profession and intend to use the successful practices of others.

I think it's critical for the successful consultant to view fees as part of a process that accompanies one's entire career. For example, you don't raise fees when times are good and lower them when times are bad, any more than you would increase marketing when times are bad and abandon marketing when times are good. Successful consultants embrace and apply pervasive strategies, not short-sighted tactics.

VIGNETTE

A member of my mentor program who successfully added professional speaking to his offerings was asked by a client to speak for one hour on each of two consecutive days in San Juan, Puerto Rico.

"What kind of a deal should I give my buyer?" he asked.

"What do you mean?" I responded.

"Well, should I give a discount for the second day, or apply it to both days? Or should I waive expenses? Or should I do one day for free if the buyer pays for my wife's expenses?"

"What kind of deal has the client requested?"

"Oh, the client hasn't asked for anything."

"Then send the buyer a bill for full fee for both days and for your expenses after the event. And keep your mouth shut except when you're actually addressing the conference."

ENTRY-LEVEL FEES

One of the worst strategies that I've ever encountered at entry level is to price low in order to get business. Since this book is for advanced consultants and flourishing practices, I won't spend too much time on this, but since early fee strategy often determines later fee levels, it's important to understand the influence (so that you can undo it, if you must).

Ironically, but completely understandably, the tendency to set low fees to attract business actually reduces business and, worse, establishes a horrible precedent that is difficult to overcome.[1]

> Poor fee strategy at the beginning of one's consulting career creates all kinds of problems later in one's career. It's easiest to reach the roof from the top floor, not from the basement.

When I refer to fees that are too low on a value basis, I mean the following: If the client would have paid, in terms of value, $70,000 for a project, and the consultant's actual fee was $58,000, that's fine. But if the consultant's fee was $24,000, that's not fine, despite "exposure," the promise of future business, or the prestige of landing that client. *That's because those factors would also have been garnered at the higher fee.*

The invidious nature of low fees early in one's career creates these problems, which must be overcome and, eventually, undone:

- The client and all the client's referral business will tend to view the investment required for the value you deliver in that type of work to be at the level you cited. Being viewed as a "bargain" is not, in and of itself, sufficient if you are not well-paid. That's not a "good deal" for both parties.
- You, yourself, begin to subliminally believe that you're at the level the market will bear for that type of value, although what you've really achieved is self-created, artificially low, market level.

---

[1]Note that since I talk solely about value-based fees, I'm not referring to fee schedules or per diem amounts when I talk about fee levels, but rather the amount of the value that the consultant is comfortable using as the basis for the fee.

- When you raise prices as a result of determining that more of the project value should be reflected in your fees, your increments will be based on a very low starting point, meaning that it could, literally, take you years to make up for the lost opportunity. It's tough for people to move fees from $50,000 to $150,000, even when the client believes the latter fee is more than fair.[2]

Early fees are not a function of one's experience (or lack of it) or limited perspective. They are a function, solely, of how the consultant educates the client, and whether or not the consultant believes that he or she is quite simply worth it.

- Your margins are much lower, preventing you from investing in the kind of marketing and promotion that builds repute and brands and that, in turn, supports still higher fee levels.
- You tend to take on too much business and the wrong kind of business to create more profit. Ironically, this actually reduces profit, since you become engaged in activity and labor-intensive work, rather than intelligent marketing and high margin work. Many would-be consultants become mired in the training business because they used training to put bread on the table, found themselves in a very low margin and price sensitive business, and sought to maximize their "billable days" rather than break out of that morass. (Subcontracting is even worse: The big "seminar houses" such as Fred Pryor and Career Track were notorious for paying as little as $300 to $400 per day. Welcome to Catch-22.)

---

[2]Professional speakers are often in worse traps when, having listened to bad advice, they find themselves at low fee levels, which can be raised slightly but would need to be tripled or quadrupled to actually bring them in line with their value. Few bureaus or clients will accommodate that degree of increase, meaning it takes years of slower increases—and lost profits— to achieve a representative market level.

That's enough on the early problems for our purposes, but it's important to lay the groundwork for what follows. We've all made mistakes, and it's important to understand how it is we came to be where we are.

TRANSITION TO "GOING CONCERN"

I love the accountants' term "going concern," which indicates that a business is, essentially, breathing, eating, and ambulatory without life support. I use the term here to indicate that, once the practice is established and the bills are being paid, there is a new phase—and new strategy—to consider.[3]

Some of you are in the "going concern" phase, because you've never bothered to market or expand your horizons so that you enter the "word-of-mouth" stage (see below). The hallmarks of the "going concern" phase are these:

- Referral business has begun and is not unusual
- About 70 percent or so of all business is repeat business
- There is still a tendency to reduce fees if competition is perceived or if any degree of buyer resistance is encountered
- Fees are about 50 to 65 percent of where they really could be, and are not methodically examined
- Some business is turned away, but not much
- The business is still far too labor intensive, and margins are relatively low

This is often the phase in which consultants don't want to "rock the boat." The problem is that, by not rocking the boat, they stay adrift, without propulsion or direction. The "going concern" should be a transient phase, not a permanent home.

---

[3]Most authorities feel that a small business has become a "going concern" after about three years, when the founder has run out of original friends and contacts and has had to generate new business to support the operation. About 80 percent of all new businesses fail within the first three years.

In this phase the consultant should begin to formulate the basics of a fee philosophy. The positions to be reconciled may include:

- What kinds of work will I encourage, what kinds will I accept, and what kinds will I phase out as unprofitable and/or unattractive?
- How can I increase my own comfort level with value pricing and educating the client about the advantages of single fees?
- To what degree can I create and offer options in almost any setting and on any project?
- What are the minimum fee levels at which I'll work?

> It's always safe to be aggressive with fees, because we almost always underestimate our value and we are competing with larger firms that must charge high amounts simply to cover their overhead. High fees can, when necessary, always be lowered (by reducing value). Low fees can seldom, no matter how much value we can demonstrate, be raised.

A rough rule of thumb is that in the "going concern" phase an aggressive consultant should be at least at the average fee levels being paid in the profession. In other words, if strategy work is being delivered for $150,000 to $300,000, then the consultant should be in the low $200,000s. See the fee progression presented in Figure 10.1.

As you can see in Figure 10.1, there are some predictable progressions that consultants go through in terms of fee practices. The idea is to accelerate or even leapfrog the intervening steps. The "going concern" phase is probably the first legitimate opportunity to do so, since entry level is really a matter of getting grounded and determining whether the profession is for you. But if you've succeeded over three years or so, and you are, indeed, a "going concern," there's no reason to laboriously advance through the ensuing phases!

On the assumption that most of the readers are in the second, third, or fourth phases, I'll continue to describe them so that you can identify yourself and plan your leap to the ultimate phase.

	Business Sources	Business Qualification	Fee Integrity	Fee Levels	Non-Consulting Fees	Margins
Entry Level	friends and former business contacts	accept almost anything	the client determines the fee	rock bottom	irrelevant; don't exist	slim to none
Going Concern	referrals and early marketing	accept most business, plan to cut out some	extreme flexibility	below average or average	probably not a factor or very low	small to average
Word of Mouth	referrals and marketing	must be high margin and strong potential	determines value-based fees and is firm	demands a premium; above average	strong fees and firm	above average
Brand	referrals, "name" in the market, and publicity	selective, only consistent with strategy	maximizes margins in every case	far above average and firm	near the top of the profession	very strong; near the top
The Ultimate Consultant	key buyers seek you out	selects only those of interest	not even discussed	at the very highest levels	not even discussed; very expensive products	extraordinary

Figure 10.1. Fee Progression Across Categories

Word of mouth means that people cite you and recommend you without any direct impetus from you at that moment. The beauty of word of mouth is that it is exponential in growth. You should, therefore, assign fees that meet the expectations of people referred to you.

TRANSITION TO WORD OF MOUTH

The word-of-mouth phase occurs when people begin speaking of you of their own volition. It may be due to the nature of work performed, or your marketing activities, or through that odd dynamic of peer pressure to which many people succumb (I can't tell you how many people have said, "Oh, yes, Summit Consulting Group—I know your work" when they couldn't possibly).

In this phase, consultants begin to apply stronger qualification criteria to potential business. Value-based fees are the norm for consulting work, and there is a conscious drive to create high margin business and not simply *more* business. The fee levels, therefore, tend to be above average for the services provided, and the quotations are firm. The consultant in the word-of-mouth phase would rather walk away from business than accept poor margin business. The need for "exposure" and potential contacts has been largely overcome by the effectiveness of the marketing effort.

At this stage of one's career, there is probably the first real opportunity to establish major retirement and investment plans, pay off long-term indebtedness, and take spontaneous vacations or make significant impulse purchases.

My experience is that word of mouth is where many consultants plateau. They begin to get "fat and happy" and complacency sets in. Even though most consultants are relatively young when they first hit this phase, their learning stops and they assume they're going to continue to grow simply by supporting the same practices that helped them get to where they are. This is the phase of the deadly "success trap," as shown in Figure 10. 2.

These plateaus can occur at word-of-mouth or brand phases (see below), but most often occur at the former, when consultants are beginning to enjoy the "good life" and assume that this is as good as it gets!

There is a key juncture when value-based fees begin to be utilized correctly and word-of-mouth recognition grows that represents a potential and lethal trap. The consultant says, "I've arrived," when the journey is only beginning to get interesting.

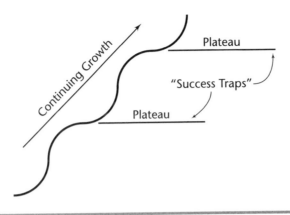

Figure 10.2. The "Success Trap" at Word-of-Mouth and Brand Phases

At the word-of-mouth phase of success, the consultant should actively seek to improve and climb the curve by:

- Creating brands around intellectual property, approaches, products, and, ultimately, the consultant's name[4]
- Further refining qualifications and selectivity for accepting new business
- Attempting to maximize margins at every single opportunity and walking away from business that does not present a "good deal" under more and more favorable terms
- Creating strong sources of non-consulting and remote consulting income, which themselves are near the top of the fee structure for their categories
- Periodically failing in attempts to attract more lucrative business and higher fees; losing out to very large concerns; learning how to best build on unique value propositions

This "middle" phase in the progression, therefore, might be the most crucial, in that it represents the stationary bike on which we think we're working

---

[4]See the second book in this series, *How to Establish a Unique Brand in the Consulting Profession* (Jossey-Bass/Pfeiffer, 2001).

out well while not really moving anywhere. Just breaking a sweat doesn't necessarily represent progress.

TRANSITION TO BRAND PHASE

In this phase, the consultant has achieved successful branding. There are actually two subsets:

1. Branding of approaches, products, methodologies, and so on
2. Branding of one's own name

Branding of Approaches, Products, and Methodologies

Examples of this subset would be The Telephone Doctor™, The Coach, The Teambuilder, *The One Minute Manager,* The Strategy Quadrant, or whatever. There is spontaneously generated publicity from sources outside consulting, which use your branded models with attribution, and from the media, which might use your approaches as readily known and quotable examples.

At this stage the consultant can be highly selective because a great many potential projects and references are in the "pipeline," many originating from the consultant's marketing "gravity" and branding, but many more resulting from the brand names themselves (for example, "Get me the guy who wrote *Managing Call Centers for Profit*"). In every case, without fail, margins should be maximized, and part of the value is in the consultant's known and accepted approaches. This puts fees far above average in the profession, with the buyer expecting as much.

Non-consulting fees can be escalated quite aggressively, since products can proliferate under an umbrella brand and others will seek the consultant out to increase product offerings.[5] Speaking fees, for example, can readily go to the low five figures.

---

[5]And, in fact, the consultant should be aware that less is more. Too much low-margin, low-value product can cheapen one's overall brand, while a few very high-margin, high-value offerings can enhance the brand and create tremendous profits.

> Branding should be done with a strategy toward involving one's name as the ultimate brand. Since this is non-duplicable by anyone else, there is no fee comparison possible at all.

There is an intermediate step that is quite successful and quite subtle in progressing from brands based on activities and products to a brand based on one's name: Create eponymous brands.

For example, "Parkinson's Laws" quickly became associated with their creator and author. Norman Augustine, CEO at Martin Marietta, created "Augustine's Laws." If you have a strategy brand that's known as "Accelerated Strategy," there's no reason why you can't migrate to "Ackerman's Accelerated Strategy" to begin incorporating your name. "The Negotiating Seminar" can easily become "Jay Randolph's Negotiations Made Easy." This can be an easy route to the second branding subset.

Branding One's Own Name

This is the most powerful brand, and shouldn't be confused with the eponymous tactic above. This is a case where Tom Peters or Peter Drucker (or Andersen or McKinsey on a corporate basis) are themselves the brand.[6]

When someone says, "Get me Alan Weiss," it means that the decision is literally yours as to whether you will accept work that is being offered to you, rather than seeking out the work or even collaborating on whether you and the buyer are right for each other. In this case the buyer is saying that the work is yours if you deign to accept it. This dynamic maximizes your margin in every case. You are very near the acme of the profession, and your margins should be near the top.

---

[6]Tom Clancy, Stephen King, and Danielle Steele have done this as authors. Virtually every actor must do it. Picasso and Warhol did it as artists. Many politicians do it, but not all. Once again I refer you to an earlier book in this series if you want to learn more details about branding in this profession: *How to Establish a Unique Brand in the Consulting Profession* (Jossey-Bass/Pfeiffer: 2001).

While the "success trap" we discussed in the prior phase doesn't represent as much of a threat here, there are two considerations in terms of fees that should be kept in mind.

First, there are, comparatively, many consultants at the product and approach branding phases, and few at the person name branding phase. My belief is that consultants who have branded their methodology and approaches tend to get "stuck" in that position and don't make the transition to personal name branding. That's why I've included the subtle transition step of eponymous naming. I don't believe you can progress to ultimate consulting unless your name becomes a brand.

Second, I don't think enough consultants seek to stretch what brands they do develop to encompass a wider and wider range of offerings. Singular brands and/or limited breadth tend to confine the consultant to a niche where learning, growth, and improved fees are not naturally forthcoming.

Consequently, I think it's important to continue to progress beyond the branding phase, no matter how lucrative and rewarding it may seem at the time.

> The ultimate consultant doesn't worry about fees and margins, similar to early in one's career, but for very different reasons.

TRANSITION TO ULTIMATE CONSULTANT

This entire series is based on achieving and reveling in a stature of the profession which I've called "the ultimate consultant." I've assigned that status as the highest level of my progression, even though one continues to grow, experiment, and benefit in this phase.

The ultimate consultant is sought out directly by buyers. There are no "middle men" or feasibility buyers. The consultants select those projects that are of most interest and mutual benefit. Fees are not discussed and may take the form of long-term retainers, deferred compensation, and other devices. The fees and margins are at the very highest of the field. Non-consulting and remote consulting fees can be whatever the consultant decides to make them.

Ironically, the ultimate consultant and the entry-level consultant both have little focus on fee levels and margins. But in the latter's case it's because business is desperately needed and there is no thought of negotiation. In the former's case, business is not needed and there is no thought of negotiation.

Relatively few may reach ultimate consulting, but that doesn't mean we shouldn't be prepared for it. People believe they get what they pay for, and it's important that we behave in a manner consistent with our value. Therefore, the ultimate consultant:

- Does not discuss fees
- Dresses and acts as a peer of high level buyers
- Is never "hired," but agrees to collaborate with the buyer

- Is known by his or her name
- Fosters products and approaches that build on name recognition
- Seeks high margin, not high volume
- Creates the aura, "Do you think we can get him?"

Where are you currently in your fee progression and career progression? The operative word is "currently." You should be acutely aware of the strategies required to progress and move ahead. Your value is increasing with your age, experience, and longevity in the business. Your fees should be increasing commensurately.

The client, competition, economy, government, methodology, project, and timing do not control your fee. You control your fee. The good news is that there is only that single variable. The bad news is that there is only that single variable.

THE BOOK'S ROI: ALAN'S AXIOMS FOR THE "GOOD DEAL"

For anyone who has taken this book off the book store shelf to glance at these final few pages, forget it. You're not going to be helped without reading the prior two hundred or so. But for those of you who have come with me this far as active participants, I'd like to make some final observations and provide some final provocations.

1. You Are Entitled to Be Compensated for Your Value

We live in a capitalist system, which works better than all others. People believe in such a system that they get what they pay for. However, the first sale is to yourself. You must believe that you are entitled to fair remuneration, and you must appreciate your own value.

Creating shared success with the client is the best way—at any time in one's career and particularly early in that career—to create shared value. The "good deal" occurs when the client believes you've been a bargain in terms of the results you've helped produce, and you believe you've been paid very well.

It is never too early to begin branding what you do, how you do it, and who you are so that perceived value is even higher. The only source for a fee is perceived value. There is no limit to perceived value and, hence, no limit to fees. The worst limitation is probably in your own mind.

2. Basing Fees on Time or Materials and Not on Value Is Simply Crazy

There is no law of supply and demand in the consulting profession. Good times and bad times economically don't matter, nor does the number of competitors, nor does your own available time. What matters is the results you generate.

The essential need in breaking away from time-based fees is to understand that your value is never a matter of your "showing up." Nor do you have to justify yourself by being in the buyer's presence. In fact, there are ethical conflicts in basing your payment on the number of times you're present.

Lawyers, architects, CPAs, and most consultants have educated their buyers incorrectly for several hundred years. Since the evidence of that mis-education is so apparent in low incomes and poor profitability, why on earth should we attempt to perpetuate it? It's up to us to educate the buyer correctly about value and fees based on that value from the initial meeting. But again, we have to believe it ourselves.

3. Buyer Self-Interest Is Based on Results

People change their behavior based on self-interest. Self-interest is most affected by results, not task, by output, not input. That's why "deliverables" are only a commodity that will be comparison-shopped by most buyers. A report, or a training session, or a coaching regimen are simply tasks performed. But improved morale, faster customer responsiveness, and more effective leadership are highly valuable organizational outputs.

Buyers will change their behavior—spend money when none is budgeted or spend more than was anticipated—not because a training session seems better but rather because customers might buy more. They're not that interested in a better interviewing procedure, but they're mesmerized by saving $300,000 a year in lower new hire turnover.

The consultant brings his or her past experiences, through an intervention, to dramatically affect the client's future. It's that final part that merits high fees, the future. The consultant's past is only an input, and the intervention is merely a device. Fees should be based on future improvement, not on past technique.

The discussion with the buyer should always be about future results, not the consultant's past or methodologies. The client's improvement will provide strong self-interest for the buyer to change behavior. The consultant's talent and devices will not.

---

4. Conceptual Agreement Is the Lynchpin

The ability to gain agreement with an economic buyer on objectives to be met, metrics to assess progress, and value to the client is the centerpiece of fee strategy. This creates a return on investment mentality instead of a cost mentality. It's critical to establish clear outcomes at a fixed investment and not to surrender to vague outcomes at clear costs.

The consultant's unique value (Why me? Why now? Why in this manner?) is also an important consideration, which is why a unique relationship with the buyer is so essential to forging trust and conceptual agreement. Measures may be objective or subjective, quantitative or qualitative, so long as both consultant and buyer agree on their reasonability and desirability.

There are some formulas to apply if you must have more comfort. But the formulas will usually depress fees and not boost them. This is art and science, and a successful consultant is adept at both aspects.

5. Existing Clients Can Be Converted to Value-Based Fees

The key here is to create a strategy based on picking selected targets that represent strong potential. Don't attempt to convert everyone, and be prepared to abandon some business.

In converting clients, offer new value, find new buyers, and find new circumstances. Make sure that existing buyers see more value in converting the relationship and/or that new buyers are educated correctly from the outset (and not by the old buyers). There is nothing immoral, unethical, or illegal about reaching out laterally to new buyers during ongoing projects.

Abandon business that you've had forever and don't know why, that isn't of sufficient margin, or that is just no longer interesting. You're doing neither your client nor yourself much of a favor in hanging on to it.

6. Retainer Business Is Discrete and Sound Business

Retainers represent access to your "smarts." Be sure that the conditions are carefully spelled out and that you're not mixing project and retainer work together. Ensure that the buyer's expectations are the same as yours.

Choose intelligent time frames with favorable fees. Organize the scope and numbers of people who have access to you. Focus on the renewal aspects, making sure there is an "overlap" to create a smooth, ongoing retainer relationship, not a succession of stops and starts.

Coordinate project work and retainer work within the same client through separate proposals and payment schemes.

7. There Are Scores of Ways to Raise Fees and/or Margins

Every day that you interact with prospects and clients, you are encountering dozens of ways to impact your fees and bottom line. Learn all the techniques you can, and build them into your conversation and promotional materials.

This might be something as simple as not disclosing any fees early in the conversation by practicing "turn around" questions to avoid being pinned down. Or it might be something as nuanced as suggesting options very early, to prepare the buyer for a "choice of yeses."

If you were to apply just two techniques a month intended to raise your fees or margins, you would probably double your profits without growing your business over the next year. If you also developed more business, you would probably increase profits by a function of four or five times. Every day you may be "leaving money on the table" by not focusing on your fee tactics.

> You have the opportunity to focus on and apply successful fee tactics every day. If you don't do this, then you have decided to reduce your margins over time. That's a heck of a way to run a business.

8. You've Heard All the Objections Already

You know what all the fee objections are, because you've heard them all before. It's criminal and negligent not to be prepared for them, not merely with rebuttals, but with effective counterarguments.

There's nothing wrong with asking about the buyer's budget—in fact, it can be a very effective tactic early in the discussion. Offering rebates will help you to acquire successive phases of a multi-phase project. Using comparisons about equipment, damaged goods, vending machines, and so on can embarrass the buyer into realizing that investments must be made in people.

Ignore the competition. The client's self-interest will serve to overcome any objections. It's not about what the competition does, it's about what you do with the buyer.

9. Non-Consulting Activities Are Lucrative

You can and should create substantial fees for speaking, coaching, products, licensing, and so on. While you may choose to ignore peripheral areas and remain a "purist," there really is no need to be so narrow.

As you succeed in the profession, it makes sense to try to reduce undesirable travel and to increase passive income so that your career trajectory is maximally beneficial to your chosen life style. Products and other "non-consulting" income streams make that possible.

Consider the options open to you and strive to create high margin products and services that place the least demand on your personal time. The more successful you become as a consultant, the easier it is to market in these areas.

10. Identify Where You Are in the Fee Progression Strategy

Consultants tend to move from an entry level stage through other, more advanced stages *if they manage their careers and their fee structures accordingly.* This doesn't happen "automatically."

Where are you in the progression, whether you use my words and standards or your own? What are you doing to prepare for the next phase? How can you tell if you've been in the present one too long already?

Unless you're growing and improving, you're losing ground. You can control your own growth and success if you create a strategy for doing so.

This book has been about achieving your life goals by helping clients achieve their business goals. It's as simple as that. It's time you began getting paid for it. That's the "good deal."

Questions to Qualify the Economic Buyer

- Whose budget will support this initiative?
- Whose operation is most affected by the outcomes?
- Who should set the specific objectives for this project?
- Who will be evaluated for the results of this work?
- Who is the most important sponsor?
- Who has the most at stake in terms of investment and credibility?
- Who determined that you should be moving in this direction?
- Whose support is vital to success?
- Who will people look to in order to understand whether this is "real"?
- Whom do you turn to for approval on options?
- Who, at the end of the day, will make the final decision?

Questions to Establish Business Objectives

- How would conditions ideally improve as a result of this project?
- Ideally, what would you like to accomplish?
- What would be the difference in the organization if you were successful?
- How would the customer be better served?
- How would your boss recognize the improvement?
- How would employees notice the difference?
- What precise aspects are most troubling to you? (What keeps you up at night?)
- If you had to set priorities now, what three things must be accomplished?
- What is the impact you seek on return on investment/equity/sales/assets?
- What is the impact you seek on shareholder value?
- What is the market share/profitability/productivity improvement expected?
- How will you be evaluated in terms of the results of this project?

Questions to Establish Measures of Success

- How will you know when this objective has been accomplished?
- Who will be accountable for determining progress, and how will he or she be held accountable?
- What information would you need from customers? In what form?
- What information would you need from vendors? In what form?
- What information would you need from employees? In what form?
- How will your boss know that the objective has been accomplished?
- How will the environment/culture/structure be improved?
- What will be the impact on ROI/ROE/ROA/ROS?
- How will you determine attrition/retention/improved morale/safety?
- How frequently do you need to assess progress? How would you assess it?
- What is acceptable improvement? Ideal improvement?
- How would you be able to prove a level of improvement to others?

Questions to Establish Value

- What if you did nothing? What would be the impact?
- What if this project failed?
- What does this mean to you, personally?
- What is the difference for the organization/its customers/its employees?
- How will this affect performance?
- How will this affect image/morale/safety/repute?
- What would be the effect on productivity/profitability/market share?
- What is this now costing you annually?
- What is the impact on ROI/ROA/ROE/ROS?

Questions to Assess Personal Value Contribution

- Why me? Can any speaker/trainer do this, or do I have special attributes?
- Why now? Is the timing particularly urgent or sensitive?
- Why is this being handled in this manner? Is there some aspect of the methodologies or relationships that is key at the moment?
- What's unique about our relationship? Does the buyer place special trust in me?
- What's my unique value added? To what extent can I "guarantee" success and exceed the buyer's expectations?

The Difference Between Inputs and Business Outputs

Here are some examples of input versus output:

Input	*Output*
• Run sales training sessions	• Improve sales closing rates
• Conduct focus groups on morale	• Improve lateral communication
• Interview former customers	• Reduce attrition rates
• Audit recruitment process	• Increase retention of new hires
• Redesign performance evaluation	• Provide higher quality, more frequent performance feedback
• Review expense procedures	• Decrease travel costs
• Improve senior officer teamwork	• Enable decision making at proper levels
• Study technological needs of service personnel	• Improve service response time of personnel

Index

59, 124; finding new buyers within existing, 83–85; given the "choice of yeses," 68–74; jettisoning bottom 15 percent of your, 126; offering new value to, 79–82, 125; offering rebates to, 126, 145–146; overcoming resistance to value-based fees by, 37–55; perpetual motion = perpetual progress of, 53–54; priorities existing, 76–79; providing full range of services information to, 120; relationships between consultants and, 11; resistance to value-based fee conversion by, 88–89; serving self-interest of, 49–51, 185–186; testing potential for shifting to value-based fees, 77–78; unique value questions to ask, 61–64, 120, 199. *See also* Business; Buyers

Coaching, 163–164

Commercially published books, 158

Comparison question, 125

Conceptual agreement, 11, 186

Consultant past-client future transformation, 51f–53

Consultant practicum: analysis of your services/products, 82; applying new value/new buyers/new circumstances, 87; reviewing promotional material, 40

Consultant-buyer relationships: aggressively marketing retainer, 107–111; capitalizing on retainer, 106–107; as foundation of value-based fee, 58–61; level of interaction in, 11; objective apportionment in collaborating, 121–122; organizing projects within retainer, 103–106; role of buyer education in, 33; sample letter of agreement for retainer, 108–109

Consultants: abandoning business concept for, 89–92; creating shared success, 14–17; fee-setting issues for, 24–27; focusing on outcomes not inputs, 38–40; impact of "billable time" on, 29–30; offering unlimited access to, 80–81; traits of successful retainer, 111; transition to ultimate, 183–184; unique value questions asked by, 61–64, 120, 199

Consulting Business Acquisition Sequence, 11f

Consulting products, 157–160

Consulting services: as art and science, 55; asking the comparison question, 125; consultant past to client future transformation of, 51f–53; "deliverables" fallacy of, 41–44; focusing on outcomes of, 38–41; measuring the unmeasurable results of, 48–49; offering options above budget limits, 119; perpetual motion = perpetual progress formula of, 53–54; pro bono, 123; providing information on full range of, 120; quantitative and qualitative measures/criteria of, 44–48; remote, 161–167;

serving the client's self-interest, 49–51, 185–186; subcontracting, 120, 124; submitting proposals for, 120–121. *See also* Non-consulting opportunities; Projects

Contingency fees, 95–96

Contracts: including provision for premium fee, 118; "plus expenses" fees included in, 118; reading the fine print on, 129; sample letter of agreement for retainer, 106–108. *See also* Proposals

Conversion factor formula, 87

Costs from Expert vs. Investment from Partner, 15f

CPAs fees, 31–32

Credibility, 13

D

"Deliverables" fallacy, 41–44

Diagnostic tools, 116n.2

Drucker, Peter, 181

E

Emotional buy-in, 10

Employee performance, 122

Entry-level fees, 172–175

Ethical issues, 24–27

Expense billing, 130

Expense reimbursement requests, 128–129

F

Fee buoyancy, 12–14

Fee objection rebuttals: filters to be overcome, 135; ignore the competition during, 148–149; importance of developing, 133–134; maintaining focus on value, 140–141; New York (direct) approach, 143; offering rebates, 145–146; overview of three, 143–145; summarizing, 149–150; utilizing "smack to the head" comparisons as, 146–148; watching for "red flags" signs, 142–143; "wedding reception" response, 143–144

Fee objections: four fundamental areas of, 134–135; "good deal" axiom on, 188; money issues, 138–139; need issues, 136–137; "red flags" to watch for, 142–143; trust issue, 135–136; urgency issues, 137–138

Fee Progress Across Categories, 177f

Fee progression strategies: entry-level fees, 172–175; "good deal" axiom on, 189; necessity of having, 171–172; "success trap" of word-of-mouth and brand phases, 179f; transition to "going concern," 175–177; transition to ultimate consultant, 183–184; transition to word-of-mouth, 178–180

Fee raising: every two years, 123–124; first fifteen techniques for, 115–118; "good deal" axiom on, 187–188; practicing, 116; preparing to, 113–114; second fifteen techniques for, 119–123; third fifteen techniques for, 123–126

Fee reductions: buyer quid pro quo in case of, 121; linking value reduction to, 118; never voluntarily offer, 117

Fee-setting: by attorneys, 30–31, 35, 67; avoid using round numbers, 116; avoiding premature discussion about, 121, 122; by CPAs, 31–32; current market fee ranges and, 124; disadvantages of time/material basis for, 26–27, 185; issues of, 24–27; for keynote speaking, 152–156; precedent set by other professionals for, 19–20; preserving client budgets and, 26; profits and time-based, 27–30; by search firms, 32–33; sensitivity to margins when, 124; supply and demand illogic applied to, 20–23, 123

Fees: alternative forms of remuneration, 167–168; clarifying "plus expenses," 118; comparing ROI from partner vs. expert, 15f; connection between value and, 115; contingency, 95–96; defining concept of, 1–2; entry-level, 172–175; how brands help, 12–14; introducing value-based, 3–5; Mercedes-Benz syndrome and value-based, 5–9; never voluntarily offer options reducing, 117; practice stating/explaining, 130; relationships between buyer commitment and, 8f; removing mention from all printed materials, 118; value-based vs. retainer, 95–96. See also Value-based fees

Ferrari brand, 12

G

Gerstner, Lou, 32

Getting Started in Consulting (Weiss), 3n.2

"Give Me a Double Axis Chart and I Can Rule the World" (Weiss subtitle), 9t

Godek, Greg, 114n.1

"Going concern" phase, 175–177

"Go/no go" dynamic, 68, 70

"Good deal" axioms: avoiding time as basis for fees, 185; buyer self-interest based on results, 185–186; client conversion to value-based fees, 187; compensation for your value, 184–185; conceptual agreement is lynchpin, 186; on fee objections, 188; on fee progression strategy, 189; on non-consulting activities, 188–189; on ways to raise fees/margins, 187–188

"Good deal" dynamic, 64–67

"Good Deal" Equation, 66, 67f

The Great Big Book of Process Visuals, or Give Me a Double Axis Chart and I Can Rule the World (Weiss), 116n.2

H

Hartman, Phil, 29n.5

Harvard School of Law, 47

"Hawthorne studies," 66

Hewlett-Packard, 44

How to Establish a Unique Brand in the Consulting Profession (Weiss), 14, 179n.4, 181n.6

How to Market, Establish a Brand, and Sell Professional Services (Weiss), 136n.3

"How to Raise Fees in Professional Service Firms" (Weiss), 114

How to Write a Proposal That's Accepted Every Time (Weiss), 16n.7, 41n.1, 71n.6

"HP frame of mind," 44

The Hunt for Red October (Clancy), 14

I

IBM, 32

Input vs. output, 201

ISBN number (International Standard Book Number), 161

J

Jones, Grace, 108

K

Keynote speaking: developing business options through, 155; establishing your value during, 153–154f; overview of, 152–153; using speakers bureaus for, 155–157

L

Late payments, 127

M

McKinsey & Co., 47

McKinsey brand, 12, 13

Margins: of entry-level fees, 174; fee-setting, 124; "good deal" axiom on raising, 187–188; product sales and, 160. See also Profits

Martin Marietta, 181

MBS (Mercedes-Benz syndrome): applied to value-based fees, 5–9; brand element of, 13; impact on perception of value, 124

Mentoring, 164–166

Mercedes-Benz North America, 43

Million Dollar Consulting (Weiss), 3n.2, 157

Money objection, 138–139

Money Talks: How to Make a Million as a Speaker (Weiss), 152, 163

Motivational speakers, 154. *See also* Keynote speaking

N

Need objection, 136–137
New circumstances transfer mechanisms, 85–87
New value: advantages of offering, 79–80; fee-raising and offering, 125; offering new access points as, 82; offering new services as, 81; offering wider access/combined buyers as, 81; unlimited access to consultant as, 80–81
New York (direct) approach, 143
Ney, Marshal, 53
Non-consulting opportunities: advantages of taking, 151–152; "good deal" axiom on, 188–189; keynote speaking, 152–156; product sales, 157–161; remote consulting, 161–167; working with speaker bureaus, 156–157

O

Objectives: establishing, 119; extending project, 127; linking value and, 119–120; questions to establish, 193. *See also* Business
The One Percent Solution, 17, 114
1001 Ways to Be Romantic (Godek), 114n.1
Outcomes: "deliverables" fallacy and, 41–44; inputs vs., 38–40
Output vs. input, 201

P

"Parkinson's Laws," 181
Passive income: "good deal" axiom on, 188–189; from keynote speaking, 152–156; from product sales, 157–161; from remote consulting, 161–167; working with speaker bureaus to produce, 156–157
Payments: advance, 126; cite U.S. dollars drawn on U.S. banks for, 130; fee schedules for, 128; incentives for one-time/full, 128; late, 127; subject to conditions of completion, 129
Perceived value, 3
Peters, Tom, 181
"Plus expenses" fees, 118
"Poor timing" excuse, 137–138
Powell, Colin, 153
Press kits: including testimonials from retainer work in, 107; place "typical results" of retainer work in, 108; removing fees from, 118
Principles of Scientific Management (Taylor), 19n.1
Pro bono work, 123
Proactive ideas, 130
Problem solving, 129–130
Process visual, 116
Product sales: guidelines for, 160–161; margin as key to, 160

Products: advantages of producing, 157–158; audiocassette tapes and albums, 159; commercially published books, 158; self-published books, 158–159; videotapes and albums, 159–160
Profits: fee-setting and basis for, 24; fee-setting and margins impact on, 124; impact of sub-contracting on, 124; product sale margins and, 160; techniques for maximizing, 131; time-based fees and, 27–30; tips on retainer fee, 102–103
Projects: advance payments for, 126; budget limitations and impact on, 119; controlling "scope creep" during, 123, 127; objectives of, 119–120, 127; offering options above budget limits of, 119; organizing within retainer relationship, 103–106. *See also* Consulting services
Proposals: citing time frame for, 126; used as confirmations, 120–121; "scope creep" response through new, 123. *See also* Contracts
Purchasing manager, 117–118

Q

QGTRIHF (What Are Your Objectives?), 119
Questions: assessing unique value, 61–64, 120, 199; comparison, 125; to establish business objectives, 193; to establish measures of success, 195; to establish value with buyers, 6–7, 197; to qualify economic buyer, 191

R

Rebates: as fee objection rebuttal, 145–146; to guarantee future business, 126
Referrals: setting your own terms following, 125; through retainer relationships, 106–107; through word-of-mouth, 178–180
Remote consulting: coaching, 163–164; described, 162–163; lucrative opportunities of, 161–162; mentoring, 164–166; situational, 166–167
Retainer fees: choosing time frames/expectations for, 100–103; defining, 95–96; optimal conditions for, 96–97; quick tips on gaining high-value/profit, 102–103; summarizing ROI of, 112; ten criteria for setting, 97–100
Retainer relationships: aggressively marketing, 107–111; capitalizing on, 106–107; consultant traits needed for successful, 111; "good deal" axiom on, 187; organizing scope/management of projects within, 103–106; sample letter of agreement for, 106–108; summarizing ROI of, 112
ROI (return on investment): axioms for the "good deal," 184–189; client need quandary and, 25; comparing expert vs. partner, 15f;

new value and revisiting, 80*f*; summarizing fee objection rebuttals, 149–150; summarizing fee-setting, 35; summarizing non-consulting income, 169; summarizing retainer fees/relationships, 112; summarizing techniques for maximizing, 131; summarizing value-based fee basics, 54–55; summarizing value-based fee conversion, 92–93; summarizing value-based fee establishment, 74; summarizing value-based fees and, 17, 24. *See also* Value-based fees